EMPOWERING WOMEN TO DO LIFE THEIR WAY
BY CREATING A PERSONAL BRAND BUSINESS.

DO IT MY WAY

DEEDRA DETERMAN

Cover and design by D2 Branding
Published in Tulsa, Oklahoma by D2 Branding

ISBN: 979-8-218-49164-2

Printed in the United States of America

To my friends and family, thank you for letting me do it my way. To my amazing, loyal team, who are much smarter than I am, and to all the countless clients who have trusted us with their marketing over the years, I am forever grateful!

CONTENTS

DO IT MY WAY

DO IT MY WAY is a philosophy I came up with that empowers women business owners and CEOs to do business on their terms with no regrets, hesitation, or fear.

Maybe you're a CEO who's worked countless hours for your company only to find yourself exhausted and not in control of your own life.

Maybe you're a female business owner who wants to be seen as the expert in your industry and get paid to consult others who wish to follow your path.

Or maybe you're an entrepreneur looking for the X-Factor in your business to set you apart from your competition.

Whichever describes you, this is your place!

There are two ways this book can and will benefit you:

1. As a complete, proven process guide. When read cover-to-cover, the chapters in this book will take you through the steps to starting and launching a new personal brand/company.

2. As a quick marketing reference tool. Maybe you already have a brand but are stuck on how to grow it? I wrote each chapter as an "at-a-glance" quick list of ideas and steps for you to follow and refer back to, according to your current specific needs.

Regardless of how you choose to engage with this book, you'll learn how to do business on your terms, by creating the life you want to live, through working the hours you want to work, and making the money you want to make!

I'm going to show you not only how to create your personal brand but also how to build your marketing plan, become a sales rockstar, grow and scale your business, and, as a result, become the best version of you!

It's time for you to DO IT YOUR WAY!

Why DO IT MY WAY?

Let me start by sharing my story and how I came up with the title, "DO IT MY WAY," for my book, podcast, and the overall theme of my life. It might sound like I'm full of myself, and it's "my way or the highway," which is untrue.

You see, I am actually not saying you need to do everything my way, as in Deedra's way (although my mom may beg to differ..I think those might have been my first words as a baby). I am a strong-willed woman, but I also know I am never the smartest one in the room. What I do know is once I started doing business on my terms, I began to see success in my life and career!

So the phrase DO IT MY WAY is actually me encouraging you to do the same: to do it *your* way.

Block out all of the noise around you from your friends, family, co-workers, and your neighbors. Whether you're a female CEO, entrepreneur, or even the CEO of your household trying to do it all...when you play by someone else's rules, it just won't work!

But, if you can figure out how to do things your way, you will live a much happier, healthier life and success will come your way. Maybe doing things your way will come by what you feel is your calling, or a spiritual direction, or even a "gut" feeling. The more I listen to my own internal voice, the more aligned I feel with myself!

Here's how this whole powerful philosophy started for me. I began my career in television, working for one of the top media companies in the world. I had to get to work by 8:30 am every day and couldn't leave until 5:30 pm -and it was even frowned upon if I left on time. TV execs were supposed to work late! I was the director of marketing, and we had a lot of success in our local market, so I was promoted to consult their other 13 TV stations across the country. During this time, TV started to dive - people were going online for news and entertainment, and they knew the industry had to change, or it would die!

I sat in countless meetings with executives talking about this wave of social media that was coming, but that's all they did to "solve" the problem—TALK! I thought if we just devised a plan and put it into ACTION quickly, we would be ok! Nothing was ever quick in corporate America. We had to have meetings about our meetings and get 50 approvals to do anything.

I always used to sit in those meetings and think, "What if we did it my way?" Let's just come up with a plan TODAY and TRY IT! What do we have to lose? Speed WINS in my book! It may not be the perfect answer, but it's better than doing NOTHING!

I am grateful for the television industry to start my career. I met so many amazing people, and I wouldn't be where I am today without that invaluable experience. However, I wasn't a fan of being in an industry that was losing market share yearly. Sometimes, God has a plan and takes you down the path without expecting it. I loved my job, but all I desired was time freedom, to work when I wanted to work, and financial freedom to make the money I wanted to make. While working my way up the corporate ladder, I was pregnant with my son, Jace, and had my two-year-old daughter, Avery, at home.

One night, I was exhausted from a long day at work. My husband was at a work dinner meeting, so I called my mom to tell her I didn't feel good. She offered to come to get Avery for the night. Then I started to have what I thought were Braxton-Hicks (mini contractions that are normal during pregnancy). But I started to monitor them and they kept getting closer and closer together. I called one of my best friends who lived across the street, and she insisted on driving me to the hospital to get checked out. My husband would meet us there. I truly thought nothing big was happening but I went in, reluctantly.

To my complete shock, the nurse who tended to me said I was dilated to a seven and rushed me to a room. I was only six months pregnant.

How could this be?

I followed all the "rules" for a safe and healthy pregnancy. I exercised daily, paid careful attention to my nutrition, stayed hydrated, etc.

So how was this happening to me?

A nurse came into my room, and I told her I thought my water was breaking. She got me a bedpan so it wouldn't make a huge mess. My husband looked down and looked back at me, white as a ghost. It wasn't my water breaking. The pan was quickly filling up with blood.

I was rushed to an operating room for an emergency C-section. I argued with the nurse, explaining I was only six months pregnant (27 weeks along), so there was no way this baby was coming.

He wasn't ready.

That's when she told me that both my life and my baby's life were in danger. We had to get him out immediately. An hour later, I delivered the sweetest, most precious 2 lbs 9 oz baby boy we named Jace. He didn't look like a typical newborn, but I still thought he was the most beautiful baby ever. If you've never seen a premature baby, especially one as young as 27 weeks, their skin looks almost translucent, showing all of their veins. To give you an idea of how tiny he was, my husband's wedding ring fit around Jace's wrist.

We were informed that Jace would have to stay awhile in the NICU. Nothing was worse than leaving the hospital without him. I remember getting in the elevator with all these happy moms carrying flowers and their newborn babies, excited to go home. I had to leave my baby there to continue to grow and develop...without me by his side.

I knew right then that my former life spent traveling and working all the time had to change.

Jace spent a total of 77 days in the NICU, and then he needed me to be home with him. My world flipped upside down. I was a planner, and this didn't fit into my plan. My corporate job, once one of the most important things in my life, didn't matter at all anymore.

The only thing that mattered was caring for my tiny baby boy and giving him the best possible care. The entire first year of his life was somewhat of a blur. We were in and out of doctor's offices every week, physical therapy, speech therapy (to learn to suck, swallow), meetings with dieticians, etc. I lived in constant fear of a diagnosis. Many babies born that early are diagnosed with Cerebral Palsy by the time they are one or two years old, and Jace displayed many of the symptoms in his first year.

After staying home for five months with him, I knew I had to give my work an answer about whether I was going to return. I proposed to work part-time at home and part-time in the office so I could still care for my son (this was before Zoom calls and working from home were common). My boss said no to my offer. They needed me full-time in the office, so I began frantically thinking of a new plan. I needed a business idea that allowed me to work for myself. I knew there wasn't an employer out there who would give me the flexibility I needed. I also had the pressure of bringing in money because we were in the middle of building our dream home.

I was considered an expert in marketing and advertising, but I wasn't sure if I wanted to dive into a business about marketing at that time in my life. I was a young mom. I wanted to spend more time with my kids at their crucial young ages, and I loved talking to other moms about mom things!
I was on a mission to figure out a business doing something I loved. I knew I needed to make a change, so I spent an entire week with a notebook, and every time I enjoyed a conversation or what I was doing, I wrote it down. At the end of the week, I discovered I could talk all day about my kids, and I loved talking to my friends about their kids! So I thought, "What if I could combine my expertise in marketing and advertising WITH being a mom?"

That's when the idea came to me to create a niche website for moms in my local area which we called 918moms.com. There was nothing out there like it.

Here was my idea: create a directory of all the schools, daycares, birthday party places, etc., in town and provide a space for moms to rate them and comment about their experiences (this was before Google Reviews). I wanted a forum on the site where moms could swap stories and share advice (this was back before moms were talking on Facebook). I wanted to create a community of like-minded moms brought together on a FREE niche website. I'd get as many moms as possible visiting this website and sell advertising to make money!

I knew the most significant buying audience was women 25-54 (moms), and who most advertisers wanted to reach. If I could get them all in one place, I knew I could sell ads, make the money I wanted, work from home, and be the mom my kids needed! I couldn't wait to get back to work and tell my friend Melanie Henry, the News Director at the TV station I worked at, about my idea! She was a working mom and struggled with long hours and being away from her family, too. She was one of the most intelligent people I had ever met. Maybe we could team up and launch a business! We were the perfect match: she was a genius at content creation, and I was the sales/marketing expert. I didn't realize it at the time, but what we built were personal brands. A website for moms, created by moms.

We didn't have an advertising budget, so we had to get creative with media partnerships to get the marketing buzz going. We talked a local radio station into letting us host a radio show called the *Mix Mom Squad*. Every Monday, we went on air for one hour to talk about fun things going around town for moms and kids! We had never been on the radio before, but we knew we could provide great content that they could sell, and we got an hour of free air time in exchange.

We knew we couldn't make any money on advertising unless we had people visiting the website, so starting with exposure was a great plan!

I remember our first show. We had friends and family call in to ask questions, because we thought no one else would! We were establishing our personal brands by becoming "experts at momming," The more moms tuned into our radio show, the more traffic we got on our website.

The more traffic we got, the more advertising I could sell! We ended up partnering with a local TV station and print publication as well to provide weekly content in exchange for the publicity. Selling advertising became easy because we could connect advertisers with the target market they were going after!

This journey began back in 2008, and to this day, I still have people coming up to me asking, "Weren't you the mom that created 918moms.com?" We only had that website for one year, but the branding has lasted over 16 years.

One of my favorite stories was when we entered our site into Tulsa's Entrepreneurial Spirit Award contest, which was started by former Tulsa Mayor Kathy Taylor. The contest had a panel of entrepreneur judges and offered a nice cash prize. We made it to the finals but didn't win. I'll never forget a judge named Sean who looked at me during my pitch and said, "Why would anyone buy advertising on a website for moms? I don't see this being a viable business."

WOW, was that the FUEL I needed to put a fire under me. I couldn't wait to prove Sean wrong! Sure enough, in one year, we had over 100,000 moms visiting the website monthly, and I was selling $70k per month in advertising for an online business with no overhead. And the winner of the Spirit Award? Well, let's just say that business never took off. I think about Sean often and am grateful for his words and how they motivated me to do BIG THINGS! Often, a setback can be followed by your most excellent comeback! Melanie and I ended up selling 918moms.com to a local media company, Griffin Media, after just one year of monumental success.

I FINALLY DID IT MY WAY!

After selling the website, I had so many people asking me to help them with their business ideas or help them navigate this new digital marketing world.

With Jace now a healthy, thriving, little boy, I was back on my feet and ready to dive full-time into marketing again. I started a digital marketing firm, D2 Branding. We specialize in Facebook, Instagram, YouTube, Google, and TikTok advertising. Our full-service agency handles website design, graphic design, video production, photography, and content creation. We have a fantastic team of digital experts who know WAY more than I do about creating websites, social media campaigns, and online sales funnels to capture leads for our clients. I'm blessed to have an incredible team who cares about our clients. We also offer business coaching services, so I get to live out my dream of helping entrepreneurs and CEOs create their own personal brands to live the life they want to live!

918moms.com would not have succeeded without Melanie and I being the collective personal brand. I didn't know it at the time, but that's what ultimately drove our success. The moms visiting and engaging with our website were women just like us. They wanted to connect with other moms and we gave them the place to do that, so it worked. If a large corporation had started a mom website in our area, it would not have worked as well. We were the faces of the business, and we had a great brand story to share, which other moms related to. Advertisers wanted moms like us to shop in their stores.

This was my first taste of how powerful personal branding can be.

Why Build A Personal Brand?

The thing I like most about personal branding is it's just YOU being YOU! You are already an expert in an area of your life, and others will pay to learn from you. You might think, "I'm no expert," but think of those things that family and friends ask you for advice about. Maybe it's your famous recipes, or perhaps you have terrific fashion advice, or maybe you're a CEO or executive who has been successful in your industry. You can take your skills, knowledge, and expertise and help those who want to accomplish what you've already done and get paid to do it! It all starts with creating a personal brand.

I have worked with many high-level executives and CEOs who have been successful and made the company they were working for millions of dollars. They made good money themselves but often at the expense of their health and time away from their kids and spouse. They weren't in control of their destiny because they were working for someone else. The owner was calling the shots, working whenever they wanted to work, and probably making three to five times what the executive was making. I remember making the television company I worked for so much money over ten years. Once I became an entrepreneur, I realized I could take those skills, package them into a personal brand, make as much money as I wanted, and work when I wanted to work!

After coaching these executive clients over the years, many took their skills and expertise and became successful speakers, authors, podcasters, influencers, or consultants, and they never turned back. You see, the beauty of working at a corporation and climbing to the top or mastering a skill over the years is you have significant experience to offer someone who wants to follow in your footsteps. That is where coaching gets really fun! There are coaches and consultants in every industry out there!

I have worked with interior designers, lifestyle bloggers, couponing moms, fitness experts, gardening experts, aerospace consultants, roofing companies, bankers, inventors, teachers, politicians, lawyers, speakers, pastors, executives, CEOs, and entrepreneurs. What a crazy variety of industries, but they all had one thing in common. They created personal brands to grow and scale their businesses!

Have you ever wondered why you are emotionally attached to some brands without an emotional connection to others? Take Nike, for example. They market greatness! They never even talk about their products. They market an emotion, a feeling!

Most importantly, Nike associates itself with a personal brand-Michael Jordan-the greatest basketball player of all time! If Nike were just a shoe company that didn't have a personal brand attached to it, you wouldn't care about them. If they only talked about how their shoes are manufactured with the best materials, no one would care.

Now, think about your insurance agent or mortgage broker. Do you care what company they are with? Not really. You care about the person helping you: their expertise, their customer service, the fact that they live by you or go to your church, or their kids go to school with your kids, and oh, by the way, you like them.

People do business with PEOPLE they like. This is why personal branding is so essential: It humanizes your business. Plain and simple.

What do the names Oprah, J.Lo, or Sara Blakely have in common? They are people who have created unique personal brands. They are household names! When you think of Oprah, you think of her as a media mogul, host of the Oprah Winfrey Show, magazine editor, actress, philanthropist, and one of the most successful black businesswomen in history. Why do those things come to mind? Because she's branded herself that way.

So, what is a personal brand anyway?

Your personal brand is the unique combination of your expertise, work experience, and personality that, together, make you who you are. It's how you present yourself to the world. It separates you from your competition and allows you to build trust with your fans or prospective clients.

Developing a personal brand in business gives you many advantages:

- People trust you more
- You have a much higher perceived value
- You are known as the "expert" in your field
- You stand out from your competition

You become a magnet that attracts clients, business opportunities, media interviews, and more! The goal is for you, personally, to become the solution to their problem. Think of it this way...When you leave a room, what do you want people to say about you? When done correctly, a personal brand presents you in your best light to those around you.

But here's the thing: people are SMART! They can spot a fake from a mile away. A massive piece of your personal brand has to do with your authenticity. You have to be who you really are! If you aren't great at real estate investing, that's probably not the personal brand you want to develop! Develop a personal brand around something you already know and love and can talk about all day!

Think of it this way. What are you GREAT at? What do other people seek you out to get advice on? In what area do you consider yourself an expert? You need to start with a clear picture of yourself and why you are doing this. YOU are best at being YOU! A personal brand is all about YOU - your talents, expertise, and brand story - the reason people want to do business with YOU!

Creating a personal brand is great but you have to make money to keep it going.

HOW ARE YOU GOING TO MAKE MONEY OFF YOUR PERSONAL BRAND? One of the greatest things about building a personal brand is building time freedom to work whenever you want and financial freedom to make the money YOU want to make! You want to build an impactful personal brand, but it must also be profitable. Will people pay you to consult them in your area of expertise? Well, you must first establish rapport. Become an expert on social media, give out lots of free content, and then ask people to buy. They will not buy from you on day one, but once they get to know you and trust you as the expert in your industry, their loyalty will show.

People trust other people more than they trust a brand itself. This is why testimonials work in business versus companies self-promoting. We live in the age of Google reviews. Everyone wants to know what everyone else thinks before they make a purchase or align with a brand! Building a personal brand helps you establish that trust.

Your Why: What is Freedom to You?

The first thing you have to think about when launching a personal brand and creating your brand story is your WHY. Why do you want to do this? If you don't know your why, you won't get very far. The biggest reason why my clients want to start their own businesses is to have freedom. Usually, they want two types of freedom: time freedom (to work whenever they want to work), and financial freedom (to make as much money as they can).

Entrepreneurial freedom is about so much more than just working for yourself. It's about being the master of your own destiny and directly reaping the rewards of your hard work. When you achieve entrepreneurial freedom, everything you earn is a direct result of the work you put into making it happen, and nothing is more satisfying than that.

If you successfully start your own business, you are on your way to achieving true freedom.

Here are the Four Freedoms that motivate the entrepreneurs I work with:

Time Freedom

You want the time you spend at work to be spent doing what you really enjoy. You also want the freedom to spend time not working, too, so you can live a full life, pour into your friends and family, and pursue hobbies that interest you. As a busy working mom, there's nothing more precious to me than time. I spent years in the corporate world with no time freedom. I worked whenever my boss wanted me to work. I felt guilty taking time off when I had a sick kid, wanted to go on a field trip or just leave early to spend some time with my family. As an entrepreneur, I've been able to achieve the freedom I need to be with my family, travel with those I love, and take care of myself. For me, time freedom is working Monday - Thursday until 4pm with Fridays off. Just leaving one hour early makes me feel like I have so much time to do whatever I want after work. And no one should have to work Fridays. That's my day to get my hair done, my nails done, run errands and just do whatever I want to do.

Financial Freedom

When you're an entrepreneur, you don't have a set salary – it's totally up to you! I remember waiting for a three percent raise from my boss every year, which was barely the "cost of living" increase...and only the very top performers even got it at all! When you're an entrepreneur, your raise is based on how much you work and the hours you're willing to put in. There's no cap on your salary because the sky's the limit. As an entrepreneur, there's really no limit to the amount of money you can make each year, because it truly ties into the effort you and your team puts forth – and that's true freedom!

Freedom with Relationships

Do you only like working with a certain type of client? Then do it! As an entrepreneur, you don't really have to work with anyone you don't want to work with.

Is someone on your team making your work more difficult? It might be time to get rid of them! You get to choose who you want to work with every day. When you're the boss, you get to be very selective with who you bring into the fold. I always choose my new team members based on their personalities – are they fun? Will they get along well with others? We have built a really great culture at D2 Branding and one bad apple can ruin it all. I know that we can teach them the skills they need to learn if they are a good fit for the team!

I remember the day I decided I only wanted to coach high-performing CEOs and entrepreneurs. I found that I was such a better coach when I was working with someone who had a highly motivated mentality and a strong work ethic. We'd mesh together so well and the results would come quickly because they genuinely listened to my advice and took action. As an entrepreneur, I had the freedom to choose which professional coaching relationships I wanted to make, and I chose to only seek out people who were highly driven like I am. True freedom is working only with the people you want to work with!

Freedom of Purpose

Entrepreneurs are the biggest contributors of money, opportunity and capability to communities all over the world, in every industry. How amazing is that?

There's no better feeling than waking up every day feeling like you're fulfilling your purpose in life. We're all born with different skills, we all obtain knowledge over the years, and we're all an expert in one area. Imagine if you could take all of your skills, knowledge and expertise and share it with the world? You could solve a problem other people are having by teaching them what you already know. That's what having a purpose is – you're not just making money, you're making a difference in the lives of others.

I decided to go into marketing because I knew it could make a difference in someone's life. I've had clients who took their spouses on trips for the first time, bought their dream home, sent their kids to private school, put money away for college and saved money for retirement — all because they created financial freedom in their business that started with powerful marketing.

Freedom is waking up, doing what you love every day, and making a massive impact on your community while doing it. What does freedom look like to you? You have to decide this before you launch your personal branding business. I always ask my clients to tell me their vision for their life before they start working with me. They lay out their exact game plan of how many hours they want to work per week and how much money they want to make each month. Then, we create a plan that fits into their lifestyle and gives them the freedom to live the life they want!

I encourage you to write down what freedom looks like to you. What would freedom with your time, money, relationships and purpose look like in your life? Once you figure this out, create a personal branding business around this lifestyle and enjoy true freedom.

Tell Your Brand Story

Now that you know why you should build a personal brand and the purpose behind your brand, it's time to develop your brand story. When I launched D2 Branding, the marketing was focused on my brand story, which was my personal journey of working in the corporate world, becoming an entrepreneur out of the desperate need for time freedom and financial freedom, launching and scaling 918moms.com to 100,000 moms and selling it within one year. In the beginning I was an agency of one, who hired freelancers to help me fulfill the client's needs, so my story made sense. Now, we have 15 people on the D2 Branding Dream Team so the story has evolved, but it took years to get there.

Here is why my story draws clients in:

I am an entrepreneur like them. I launched my business without any money so I understand the stress that goes into launching. Many of my clients are parents too, and they understand the need for time freedom and it's their goal to have work/life balance. They understand I had to hustle to get my business off the ground so I understand sleepless nights. And rather than just owning "another marketing company," my clients know I can empathize with them on the trials of entrepreneurship because I've launched and sold my own business.

Oh, and by the way, I'm also a marketing expert and a business coach so even clients who don't pay for coaching, end up getting free advice when they work with us. I spent 10 years in traditional media, then saw the power of digital marketing and grew a massive website quickly through the power of social media. Most of our clients are frustrated with the decline of the traditional media audiences and they are looking for a digital solution so we are a great solution for them. My brand story is what helps clients have an emotional connection to D2 and it provides credibility in our industry. The first thing I do in my coaching sessions is create a client's brand story.

I know it can be scary to launch a personal brand, put yourself out there and tell your story! I launched a personal brand without realizing I was launching a personal brand. I was all over the radio, television and print that year we started 918moms.com. I never launched thinking I wanted to be the "face" or the "expert mom" but it made branding the website really easy. So think about this: What knowledge do you have to share with others to make an impact in their lives?

I have worked with personal brands for years. From TV personalities, to politicians, to big time entrepreneurs and CEOs- all of them are uncomfortable when I first tell them they need to put themselves out there: What will other people think? You can't think about what other people will think. You have to think of the impact your story will have to help other people. You have a specific audience you are going after that wants to learn from your experience. It doesn't have to be everyone! Oh, and you can make money doing it!

Let's say you don't have a personal brand, but you own a business. You still need to create a brand story. A brand story takes your company a step further. Instead of just being a normal business like any other, you are presenting your business as real people with a real story, inspiring an emotional connection to your customers. This will definitely set you apart from your competition.

Think of Whole Foods compared to Albertsons. Both companies sell groceries, but Whole Foods relates to its audience with the slogan, Our purpose is to nourish people and the planet.

Rather than just talking about their groceries, Whole Foods has a purpose-driven mission that sets the standard of excellence for food retailers. They make it known that things like environmental stewardship, community giving and responsible sourcing are just as important to them as their products. Their marketing message shows that Whole Foods cares about their customers and the environment. People whose values align with Whole Foods identify with the company and they feel good about spending their money there. They have an emotional connection to Whole Foods and its mission, whereas they may feel indifferent to a grocery store like Albertsons. Although both companies sell groceries, only one of them is telling a brand story, which has helped to make them very successful.

Every company has a story and a purpose behind what they do.

If you don't have a brand story, now is the time to get to work. Here are six steps to creating a brand story that your customers or clients will love:

1. Start with your company name. Why did you choose this name? Does it have significant meaning that would be interesting to your customers?

2. Describe what you do as if you were talking to someone who has no knowledge of your business or industry. What problem are you solving for your customer? Is this a problem you had and that was the reason you created this business?

3. What do you want your customers to feel when they come into contact with your brand? I always tell my team that I want our customers to think we are the experts in our industry but also know that we're a fun team. People do business with people they LIKE! How do you want to relate to your customers? How do you want them to describe you?

4. What is your vision for the company, or your why? Why do you do what you do every day? This has to be greater than just to make money. If you're starting your business just to make money and don't have a greater purpose, you'll burn out quickly, and your customers will see right through it. Tell your customers why you do what you do.

5. What is your X-factor? What makes you stand out from your competition? You need something that sets you apart from other companies, giving you an advantage. Remember D2 Branding's X-factor is providing business coaching along with digital marketing solutions. What do you do that is different from the rest?

6. Who is your dream client, or your ideal audience who you want to identify with your brand? Remember, there are riches in niches, meaning that you don't need everyone to buy from your brand, just your ideal niche. Pick a niche and speak to that niche. All of your marketing messaging should be tailored to your dream client.

Now that you have the steps to creating a company brand story, get your team together, answer these questions and start to write your brand story in an interesting, memorable way! A brand story tells everyone your motivation for starting your business, why you get up and do what you do every day, why customers should care, and why they should trust you, like you, and buy from you! Everything you do should incorporate this brand story.

Why the Entire Marketing Mix Matters

I realize when you first launch your personal brand, it may not be feasible to do the entire marketing mix. You may just be able to create your logo and social media pages, which is a great start. Start branding yourself and show up on social media as the expert educating your audience, offering tips and tricks in your industry, and giving free advice to establish credibility. However, when you have the entire marketing mix working for you, that is when the magic happens!

What do I mean by the entire marketing mix? It is everything that is created to bring your brand to life on all platforms. It captures who you are with a logo, professional photos, brand story video, website, social media pages, branded presentations, consistent brand messaging, content creation and an entire strategic marketing plan. Everything you need to look like an expert, capture leads and get sales.

I have worked with many clients who spend thousands on their logo, website, brand story video and then have zero dollars to market. How is anyone going to find you if you don't do any marketing? First you have to create your assets, then you have to market to get sales. You can't stop at the creation process and you can't market with creating first! At D2 Branding, we have a 6 step process before we work with brands. If you go out of order, it gets messy and does not work.

First, we evaluate the brand and then we do marketing research in that industry. We evaluate the logo, website, social media presence, videos, photography, content, and marketing strategy. Then, we start to strategize a plan based on the client's goals. Next is to create any assets that are needed (logo, website, brand story video, social media presence, etc). THEN we are ready to market. There is no use marketing a terrible website, yet people do it all of the time. They spend marketing dollars driving traffic to their website that has no call to action, customer testimonials, or anything needed to convert prospects into buyers. We then consult you on how to get a return on your investment. Most marketing companies don't even mention ROI (return on investment) because they don't want you to hold their feet to the fire when there is no return. As a business coach, I am always looking for a return. It doesn't matter how many hundreds of thousands of impressions you get with your ad if you don't have any sales.

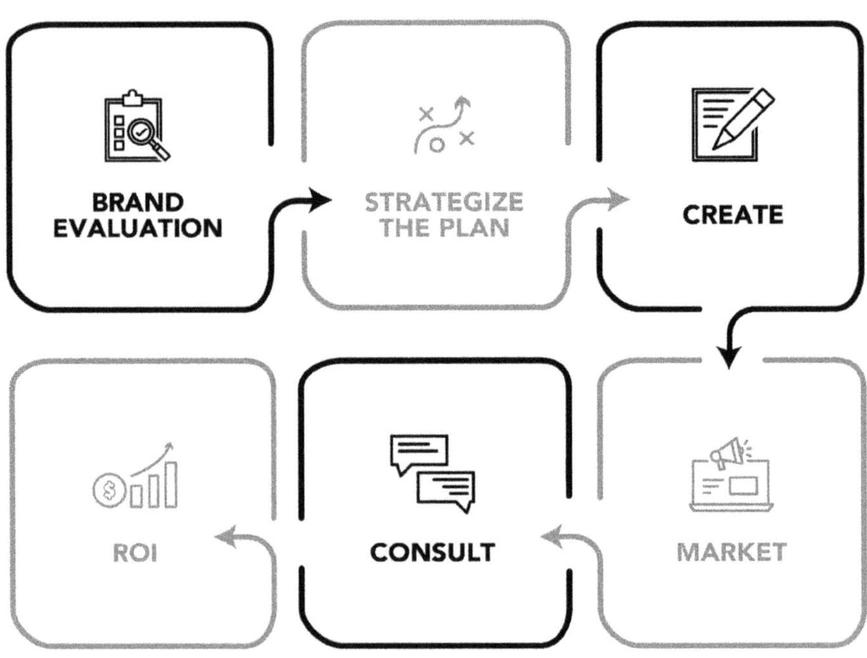

One of the most fun clients we have worked with is Sugar Llamas. Sugar Llamas is a brick-and-mortar location that offers delicious cake donuts, gourmet coffee and ice cream in a fun atmosphere. The owners came up with the concept and didn't have much competition in the market with their products. Yummy sweet treats for the kids and gourmet coffee for mom and dad. They also did extensive research finding the perfect donut making machine, unique ingredients, gourmet coffee, and amazing ice cream. D2 Branding was honored to do all of their branding and marketing for the launch. We pitched personal branding to them, but they were not interested in being the "face" of the company, so we created a mascot, a Llama, which developed the name "Sugar Llamas!" D2 Branding created their logo design, website design, marketing videos, and photography. We kicked off their grand opening with a digital marketing ad campaign on Facebook and Instagram giving away Free Coffee and Donuts for a Year. The goal was to build a massive list of people interested in mini donuts and gourmet coffee that lived within a 5 mile radius of their store. We were able to get over 3,900 names, phone numbers and emails of people entering the contest in only 30 days! This was HUGE for them to have an audience to market to very quickly! They were qualified candidates because you aren't going to enter a contest to win mini donuts if you don't like donuts! We followed up by announcing the winner through an email and text campaign and offered everyone who didn't win a BOGO offer of "Buy 6 mini donuts and get 6 free for a limited time!" The "free food" offer had urgency to act now. Who is going to pass that up? When we met with the owners after launching to go over their stats, they were so excited because their numbers exceeded their projections dramatically after they'd only been open for about a month. They couldn't believe their success - but I could, because they did everything right with their launch. They created the entire marketing mix! They created an amazing brand and had an ideal marketing strategy that resulted in quick growth. Oh and by the way, they had a killer product!

The reason they had such great success with their launch comes down to these three factors:

1. They were able to create a product that people want. Everyone loves food – especially sweets. The key to marketing is either bringing people pleasure, or presenting a way to get them out of pain, and nothing brings people more pleasure than enjoying a yummy sugary treat. It's all about having a great product. You can do all the marketing in the world, but if your product doesn't live up to the expectations of your customers, you're likely to lose them. They didn't just create any donut, they created cute mini donuts with yummy toppings and gourmet coffees for the parents.

2. They invested in a complete marketing package. D2 Branding was able to create a memorable brand for them incorporating a llama. Who doesn't love animals and llamas aren't used everyday in marketing. It's unique. It stands out. The logo is fun and friendly and looks great on their signage, hats and tshirts. We created a fun, easy-to-navigate website. Additionally, we produced professional photos and videos for their assets and launched a comprehensive social media ad campaign on Facebook and Instagram with an irresistibile offer. It doesn't matter how great your product is if you don't have good marketing to pair it with, because if no one knows about your business, they're not going to buy your product. I always say it's not the best product that wins, it's the best marketing that wins! You want people to stop in their tracks when they're scrolling through social media and pay attention to what you're saying and offering. Then, they'll become familiar with you, start to like you, and decide to come to your location and give your product a try. We had the pleasure of creating Sugar Llamas' entire brand look and all of the accompanying creative elements with the goal of capturing a list

of potential customers we could market to in the future - we ensured this by having people enter the contest by providing their names, phone numbers and email addresses. This did two things:

1. We have their data to continue to text and email them other specials.
2. We captured their IP addresses once they visited our landing page, which meant we can follow them online with ads.

It is a "warm" audience because they have already entered a contest and are familiar with the Sugar Llamas rather than going after cold traffic that has no idea who we are and maybe they don't even like donuts.

In the first 30 days of launching the Sugar Llamas campaign, we had 3,946 people sign up for the contest and the ad was seen over 220,000 times, resulting in a 2x return on our ad spend with their redemptions in-store.

We then followed up with a video campaign that shows close-up shots of their amazing treats. In only two weeks, over 8,500 people who live in a 5 mile radius of their store have viewed the video, with us spending only two cents per view. Truly, there's not a more cost-effective way to market. This approach worked so well because it allowed us to stay at the top of the minds of the people who had already shown interest in Sugar Llamas by clicking on the ad. In marketing, you want to get in front of the potential customer repeatedly until they react to what you're trying to sell them. This way, they go from being unfamiliar with your brand to familiar. Once they're familiar, they will start to like you, trust you and buy from you with time. And then you've got to have great customer service in-store which leads to repeat customers.

Once a new customer comes to your location or visits your online store, you need to wow them with customer service and provide them with a great experience so they'll want to return. Remember that people choose where they shop and do business, so it's important to make them want to come back (and tell their friends)!

Having a complete marketing mix (having a great product, investing in marketing tools, providing excellent customer service) is the key to having a successful business. These factors are all of the things the customer will think of when they're deciding if they'll buy from you. This means that your logo, website, social media, videos and in-store experience should all align and look cohesive. All areas of your business must be operating on the same cylinder to succeed. This is very important to remember when launching your personal branding business.

What Do I Post on Social Media?

If you don't have a budget to do the entire marketing mix, a great place to start is with your social media. Content is king and helps establish you as an expert, a credible source, but content can be overwhelming. You are trying to run your business and the last thing you have time for is creating daily content. The question I get asked the most is, "What do I post on my social media?"

It's difficult to create content every day that's relevant to your customers. But, here's the first thing I would do: Make a content calendar of holidays, special events and promotions your business will run throughout the year. For example, are you offering a Mother's Day special or a Black Friday deal? Or, maybe it's national sushi day and you own a sushi restaurant – you should definitely have a post about that! Another recommendation I have is posting on your social media three to five times a week, and since every day isn't a holiday or special occasion, you need to find other engaging ways to fill your feed.

If you don't have a graphic designer on staff, I would recommend downloading the Canva app. It's a great tool to create graphic templates that match your branding colors, font, etc. It's an easy-to-use, simple tool to create fun graphics for social media.

To fill the space on your social media pages in between major holidays and promotions, I came up with 16 ideas for potential social media posts.

POST TYPE	STRATEGY/PURPOSE	BENEFITS
VIDEO	•Share information •Entertain	Eye-catching videos stop people from scrolling and promote engagement with your brand.
LIVE VIDEO	•Show off your authentic self •Reach a lot of people without spending money •Familiarize people with your brand	Facebook and Instagram reward you for going live and will promote your video, boosting your chances of gaining followers.
STAFF PROFILES	•Introduce your audience to your people	The more people feel like they know your company and its people on a personal level, the more likely they are to buy and share with others.
COMPANY NEWS • AWARDS PRODUCT LAUNCHES	•Position your audience as "first to know" about new products and services	People love to feel like they're "insiders." Loyal followers are more likely to share your brand with others.
MARKET DATA	•Position yourself as industry expert by sharing your skills, knowledge and expertise	People buy from brands they trust. If your audience believes you're the expert, they will buy from you.
ARTICLES BLOG POSTS	•Drive traffic to your website	When you share articles & blog posts on your website, it drives traffic via SEO. When you share these on social media, you are continuing to drive web traffic & promote purchasing!
BEHIND-THE-SCENES	•Build brand authenticity	Organic content creates a sense of trustworthiness in your brand creating connection between you and potential customers.
CONTESTS	•Give your followers a reason to interact with your brand	Contests and giveaways boost engagement and help you gain followers when you ask people to like/share for a chance to win a prize.

POST TYPE	STRATEGY/PURPOSE	BENEFITS
INFLUENCER COLLABS	•Align yourself with someone who already has access to your target audience	When influencers share your brand, you add another level of authenticity because someone they trust is saying they love your product or service.
PRODUCT PHOTOS BEFORE & AFTERS	•Show tangible examples of what you offer or the difference you can make	Followers love visuals! Show them your products, services, etc. in away they can relate to.
USER-GENERATED CONTENT	•Show followers how liked you are by other real-life people	When other people share how much they love your brand you'll gain followers from their followers. New followers = new customers
INSTAGRAM STORIES	•Share unfiltered/edited content of the "here and now" for your business	Many users click through stories rather than scroll posts. This is another way to promote your brand to followers.
INTERESTING/ INSPIRATIONAL QUOTES	•Entertain followers with enjoyable quotes that align with your brand	People love reposting quotes on their own pages. This is a great way to redirect people back to your page.
GUEST TAKEOVER	•Surprise followers with a fun change of pace on your feed	Let an employee take over your social account for a day. People love to see different personalities and fun new content.
TESTIMONIALS	•Brag on yourself using text or video testimonials from past and current happy clients	Build credibility by highlighting clients' own positive experiences with your brand.
AUDIENCE QUESTIONS	•Get ideas for content from your audience	Boost engagement and authenticity by asking followers what content they want to see on your feed.

The next time you feel stuck while trying to schedule social media posts, refer to this chart!

Stop Selling and Start Talking on Social Media

Social media can be daunting and can feel like another task on your to-do list as a business owner but it is one of the most important things to do when you are building your personal brand. Most entrepreneurs don't have the time to spend all day coming up with creative ideas for their social media accounts. They might only have 15 minutes a day to post something, so their first instinct as entrepreneurs is to try to sell something online. They create a call-to-action post that encourages people to sign up for something or take advantage of a deal they have going on with their product or service. The problem with this approach is that to social media audiences, posts like these feel like white noise. They feel like a car dealer yelling at you on TV, advertising his latest sale. As business owners, we have to offer value on social media to get people to listen. A customer has to get to know you, like you and trust you before doing business with you. If all you're doing on social media is selling, people won't listen.

Gay Vee talks about this concept in his book *Jab, Jab, Jab, Right Hook*. He writes, "You have to offer so much VALUE that when they are ready to buy what you are selling, they will feel guilty not using you!"

Jabs are meant to offer value — they make you laugh, entertain you or offer advice — while right hooks are your call-to-action posts. You need to offer 3x the value on social media to offset your one ask. Here are five ways we offer value to our clients and prospective clients at D2:

1. The *DO IT MY WAY* podcast. We've been recording this podcast for a few years now and continue to get great traction because we offer free marketing advice. This advice is great to post on our social media and drive traffic to our podcasts, which often lead to prospects inquiring about D2 Branding's service. We are educating and offering advice, not trying to sell.

2. Email marketing. Some of the best content can be sent to the VIPs on your email list! If you offer them something valuable, they will start to get to know your brand. Don't always make your emails sales attempts. Offer valuable content so they get to know you, like you and trust you. Our emails feature real life marketing examples and cover topics that contacts on our list can learn from.

3. Blog posts. Blog posts are a great way to offer value on your website and also increase your SEO rankings with Google. The more content you have on a particular subject, the more Google will push your website to the top when someone in your area is searching. Blog posts can be pushed out on your website, in your email marketing and on your social media.

4. Social media is the perfect place to add value. You are the expert in your area, so share insider tips and tricks, discuss industry trends and share case studies from things you have done in your business or even a case study you read about on an industry website. You are the expert sharing expert advice.

5. Speaking is another great way to give value to your

prospects. Offer to speak at an industry conference to be seen as an expert and walk away with hundreds of people who know who you are and who you can market to and follow up with. Invite them to join your email list for free or give away a free e-book they can download if you get their name, phone number and email.

Offering value is a great business strategy, regardless of what industry you're in. Your focus should be on repurposing your content so you can push it across all platforms. For example, when I create a podcast, we turn the same topic into a blog post, an email newsletter, a TikTok video and Facebook and Instagram posts. I only did the "work" once, but turned it into great content for all of my audiences to access and enjoy across all platforms.

So the next time you want to go on social media and sell something, step back and think of some value you can offer instead. A great way to come up with content ideas is by thinking back to where you were in your career five years ago. What problems did you have? How did you overcome them? How can people learn from your mistakes?

To recap, on social media, you want to Jab, Jab, Jab, Jab, Right Hook. It's like a conversation with your best friend – offering value and advice and not expecting anything immediately in return!

What will you do this week to offer value to your clients and prospects on social media?

Five Marketing Moves to Double Your Revenue Now!

I'm all about keeping it simple when it comes to marketing. Here are five easy marketing moves to help you double your revenue right away!

1. Invest in Search Engine Optimization.
Your website needs to come to the top of Google when people search for key terms in your industry. 85% of people search Google before they do anything; whether it's buying a house, deciding where they'll go on vacation or searching for an HVAC company to fix their air conditioner. You name it, people are searching for it. When you invest money in an SEO strategy that gets your company's website to the top of Google, it's guaranteed that you'll get calls and leads coming in. Most of these leads will be qualified because if someone is searching for your service, they already want what you have to offer.

2. Start a referral program.
There's no better lead than a lead who comes from a trusted source. For this reason, you need to have an influx of referrals from current or past happy clients. Much of our business at D2 comes from happy clients referring their friends and family members to us. These referrals are likely to do business with you because the recommendation is coming from a trusted source. If you don't

have a referral program in place, this is an affordable way to increase your bottom line using your current or past customers.

3. Take advantage of digital marketing.
You need a presence in the digital space, period. Whether you like social media or not, you can't beat the reach you can get online. You can reach thousands of people with a simple post, which is a much quicker and more effective way to reach new clients than traditional media. Using social media allows you to connect with your audience and build familiarity. Only good can come from building up your business's social media presence.

4. Create a seamless lead nurture process.
It's important to have a great system in place to nurture the leads that you'll get from Google, referrals and social media. Lead nurturing is essential because not everyone will buy from you the first time you talk to them; especially if your product or service is expensive. I've had people come back to D2 and want to work with us a year after I initially reached out to them. A great lead nurture process is email marketing. A client needs to know you, like you, and trust you, in order to buy from you—and this process takes time. An email sequence helps your potential client become more familiar with you; and if you can offer them some value (like in an informative monthly newsletter); they'll grow to trust you, too.

5. Always upsell.
The easiest way to increase your revenue is to get more money from the customers who are already paying you. What else can you offer them that will make their lives easier? You need to have a front-end offer to get them in the door, and a back-end offer once they're there. At D2, we use website design as a front-end offer to get customers in the door. Once we create a website for them, they need something to drive traffic to the web-

site. That's when we pitch social media content posting, search engine optimization and digital marketing as our back-end offers.

If you're looking to double your revenue and don't know where to start, try these five marketing ideas!

Why Building a List is GOLD

One of the most important things you can do when starting your business is building a list of customers and potential customers. This list can consist of anyone and everyone who's ever visited your website, bought something from you, come to your booth at a trade show or listened to your podcast. Lists can be very powerful tools, yet, I talk to entrepreneurs every day who haven't built one for themselves. They might have a list of past and current customer information, but what about those potential customers who clicked on Facebook ads or visited the company website but haven't bought yet? To go after that customer and make a sale, you need to build a list and market to them!

The people on your list are your potential customers who need to know you, like you, and trust you, before they buy. These are the ones who are just getting familiar with you. Put them on a list, so you can market to them. Now you've set up a system that sets them up to get to know you and your business better.

Here's an example I shared with one of my coaching clients recently. Let's say you're a business owner who ran ads for your business on TV every day for an entire year. This strategy may not be the most effective one, and here's why: TV ads are expensive, and you can run a hundred ads, yet obtain no data on who actually watched those ads. So how can you know who to target again? You can't. Because what traditional advertising lacks is the ability to capture IP addresses (to deliver ads to), email addresses (to send newsletters to), and phone numbers (to send text campaigns to).

With digital ads, however, you can automatically build lists. Digital advertising allows you to capture names, phone numbers and email addresses with lead generation campaigns, as well as IP addresses, without the prospect even having to input their information. You can install a pixel on your website and on your ad's landing page which captures the IP address of anyone who clicks on them – meaning you can deliver another ad to them any time.

Research says it takes seven to eleven times, on average, of getting in front of a potential customer to convince them to buy from you. You've probably seen this happen to you without even realizing it. You go to buy a cute pair of new shoes online, then end up changing your mind or getting distracted, so you don't go through with the purchase. The next thing you know, you're seeing ads for those shoes everywhere – it's like they're following you around! The pixel captured your IP address when you clicked on the shoes and now it's firing off more and more ads until they convince you to buy. There's really no better prospect to follow online than someone who has already shown interest in what you have to offer – it's brilliant marketing!

We've been running digital ads for our clients for years. Those clients have built up massive audiences by doing this, meaning they have long lists to target. These lists are composed of the people who already know them, like them, and trust them, so they react quickly to the ads.

The same principles apply to in-person events. I was pitching our services to a real estate agent the other day who had been in business for 20 years. He hadn't done any online marketing but was very well-known in town. Over the years, he'd hosted hundreds of open houses, thus crossing paths with thousands of prospects. I asked him how long his list was, and he looked at me like he had no idea what I was talking about.

Just think: If he had created a simple drawing for some sort of prize at each one of his open houses over the years, he could have captured thousands of potential clients' names, phone numbers and email addresses. That's 20 years' worth of people who could have bought and sold several homes with this agent, had he only captured their information and marketed to them over the years. This simple (and super low-cost) strategy would have positioned him as a "top-of-mind agent," so when people were ready to buy or sell a home, they would immediately think of him.

Maybe you're looking to build up a business and sell it one day. The potential buyer will look for these three things:

1. Your net revenue.
2. What processes you have in place to duplicate and scale your business.
3. The size of your potential customer list.

When we sold 918moms.com, the whole reason we were able to sell was because of our list. We had 100,000 moms in the Tulsa area on our website – a massive amount of potential buyers for their advertisers. Our revenue was substantial – we were making $70k a month from advertisers with little overhead – but that number wasn't that important to them. They wanted our list!

Here are five reasons you need to build a list:

1. You can quickly reach large quantities of people who are familiar with you to market a new product or service.
2. You can personalize your messaging.
3. You have control over your list – it's yours and can be used for years to come. If all of your followers are on Facebook or Instagram, a platform you don't control, they could be gone tomorrow.

4. It's a great way to build trust.
5. If you are looking to exit your business and sell, your list is HUGE for the potential buyer.

Whether you're just starting your business or are someone who's been in business for 20 years, now is the time to start building your list!

Increase Your Profit With Customer Testimonials

Have you ever been chatting with your girlfriends about your favorite brand of makeup or the most comfortable workout shoes you just bought? Notice what they do after – immediately go online and check it out for themselves! After all, customer reviews are the absolute best referral for businesses. You're going to trust your friend who's already tried out the item for herself and given it her approval, before you buy. When it comes to your business, customer testimonials always work better than you telling people how great your own product or service is. People trust other customers' opinions over yours, because the opinion is authentic and the customer has nothing to gain from it. They're genuinely sharing their experience and telling people how much they enjoyed it. Customers like to hear from other customers, not from the brands themselves, what working with that brand or buying from them is like.

People need to get to know you, like you, and trust you before they buy from you. Customer testimonials are the easiest way to build that trust. Customers don't just want to know that you can solve their problems. They want to know that you can do it better than anyone else can!

So, how do you get customer testimonials?

My favorite way to present testimonials is through videos. Most reviews that you see are text, but statistics show video is actually much more effective and impactful. It's easier for people to consume and it generates more shares on social media, which helps you reach a larger audience. Importantly, videos are seen as being more trustworthy, since it's hard to "fake" a review on video. You can even film these with your iPhone – in fact, that might even make it feel more authentic! The best time to capture a testimonial is when you're making your final delivery to a client. For example, if you're a commercial construction company, you could easily take your phone out when you're having the final reveal of a new building with a customer. There would be no better time than when they're seeing their amazing new building for the first time, to get a short clip of their testimonial. Then you can use the video in future sales presentations, on your website, on social media, in e-newsletters or emails.

Here are five ways to get testimonials for your marketing:

1. Ask your customer if you can take a video of them talking about their experience with your product or service. You only need to ask one or two questions, and it can be very casual. The more 'off the cuff' it is, the more believable it will feel.

2. If video isn't an option or the customer isn't willing to be filmed, have them text you or send you an email answering a few questions about your work.

For example, at D2 we ask a clients:

"What was your business's biggest problem before you started D2's marketing?"

"What results did you gain from our marketing campaigns – how many customers bought from you?"

"What was the return on your investment of marketing dollars spent?"

"Would you recommend D2 Branding to others?
If so, why?"

3. Ask your clients to submit Google reviews, Facebook reviews, LinkedIn recommendations, Yelp reviews, or even YouTube reviews. I highly recommend getting Google recommendations because they help index your company when people are searching for key terms in your industry. If someone is searching for a company like yours in your area, and you have a lot of Google reviews, you're more likely to come up closer to the top of the page. The conversion rate here is often very high because the potential customer has already made up their mind: they want what you have, you just have to convince them that you're the best option for the job!

4. When you receive a compliment from a customer by phone, text or email, ask them if you can use it as a testimonial! I always ask them if they mind texting me what they said so we can use it as social proof on our website, and they're usually happy and willing to do so.

5. Ask for feedback on your social media channels! This is a good way to learn how your company is doing and capture reviews you can use. Don't be afraid to ask.

6. Client testimonials create deeper emotional connections with your brand. They're easy to get, don't cost you any money, and are extremely powerful in marketing conversion. What are you waiting for?

Why You Must Show ROI in Marketing

ROI, or return on investment, is an essential part of marketing, because it allows you to see which areas of your strategy are working and which are not.

If you're a business owner, it's imperative to know exactly where your customers are coming from. This is the only way you can tell if your marketing is working.

The areas where you're seeing a great return are where you should continue to pour your budget into. For example, if you're reaching more customers by using social media giveaways on Facebook and Instagram, you should continue to invest time and money into building up your presence on those platforms.

To track your ROI, it's crucial to communicate with your customers and ask what brought them to you. There are several ways I recommend doing this: You can create a simple form that a customer must fill out when they visit your website, or, you could ask your receptionist to ask each customer who walks in how they heard about your business and record their answers on a Google sheet. These simple practices aren't time-consuming but can be a game-changer in your business.

When you talk to customers directly and ask them how they found you, you'll no longer waste money by guessing which part of your marketing strategy made them choose your business.

It's also worth it to consider those in your network who may be referring business to you. Are there friends or former colleagues of yours who are sending customers your way? Connect with them and find a way to thank them for the extra business. At D2, we pay our referral partners. It's an easy gesture to thank them for trusting D2, and most of the time, they'll continue sending us business.

If you've never tried tracking your ROI before, now is a good time to start. In this day and age, we have so many different channels for reaching new customers: social media advertisements, Google campaigns, influencer marketing, referrals... the list goes on!

Here's how I recommend keeping track of your ROI:

Take the sales growth from that business or product line and subtract the marketing costs from that number. Then, divide that number by the marketing costs. Multiply that total times 100. For example, if your sales grew by $1000 and you spent $100 on marketing, you'd end up with a total ROI of 900%. ROI is so important because it removes all of the guesswork from your marketing. It can also be useful for other areas of your business, like calculating the return on investment for a new employee or a new software purchase.

It's important to point out that your marketing ROI should be calculated every month, but it can also take months to see a return. For that reason, you can't use a new marketing strategy for one month and then cancel it when you don't see a return.

I usually advise people that three months is the minimum time needed to track ROI and see how your marketing is performing. After the three month mark, you should start to see your stats trending upwards and your campaigns gaining traction. It might take a few more months to see a complete ROI, but if you're trending in the right direction, you're on track to success.

Why You Can't Stop Marketing

Potential clients often call me and ask, "How long do I need to run my marketing campaign? Can I do a campaign for six months and stop?"

My reply is always simple: Do you want to stop selling your product or service? Of course not. This means you have to continuously market, if you want to continuously make sales.

It's important to remember that top-of-mind awareness is a real thing. If your product or service is in the mind of a potential customer and it solves a problem for them or brings them pleasure, they will buy.

I'm actually the perfect example of this phenomenon. I'm a busy mom as well as a business owner, so I don't have much free time to shop. Instead, I scroll my Instagram feed. If I see something cute, I swipe and buy (especially if they target me with ads and I see the item over and over). This method is simple and easy to use, and with one click, I'm on my way to a new outfit. If I'm a frequent buyer, the website has my credit card info saved, so it's one click, and I buy! Think about it: If I hadn't seen that ad on Instagram over and over, I likely would have never made the purchase.

Car dealers are another great example. Do you ever wonder why they never stop advertising? Because it works! I'm sure we can all think of two or three car dealers in our city that are constantly running advertisements. If they weren't getting a return, they wouldn't advertise.

I know in my local market, some car dealerships spend up to $100,000 a month on ads. This is because if they stop, they risk losing market share, and no longer have top-of-mind awareness in the market. Then competitors can slide in with their advertising to become the one potential customers think of next time they are in the market to buy a car.

You should consider marketing the same as paying your mortgage or utility bills. You can't not do it. It's a monthly budget just like turning the lights on in your workspace. You can't live without it!

A question I get asked all of the time is, "Once I get to the top of Google, can I stop doing search engine optimization?"

The answer is no! SEO is a long-term play, and Google should be your number one referral! If you come to the top of Google for key terms in your industry, you win. You will definitely get calls from potential customers because 85% of people search Google before they make purchases.

When you get to the top of Google, but stop developing your SEO, you'll drop. It won't happen overnight, but just like it takes time to get to the top, you'll gradually start dropping until your competitors pass you by. For these reasons, SEO has to be something you continuously work at - trust me, it's worth it.

My biggest referral for D2 Branding is Google. Referrals from Google are actually my favorite leads that come in because they've already determined ahead of time that they have a need we can fill.

Think about outbound marketing efforts such as Facebook, Instagram or TikTok ads. You can deliver your ad to a highly targeted audience, but you don't know if they actually need your product or service right now; you're just hoping they click. You can target a specific audience, but you need more leads through outbound marketing to get sales. With Google search, you already know they want what you have because they're out there looking for it. They just might not know about you yet, so it's an easier sell.

If SEO is not in your marketing plan, it absolutely should be, because Google isn't going anywhere. SEO is not an overnight marketing solution - it's a marathon, not a sprint. It can often take months to get to the top of Google for key terms in your industry, but once you start to land at the top, you'll get tons of calls from potential clients.

The same rules apply for social media content posting. It's important to have an active social media presence for your business. If you stop posting, your business will stop existing in the eyes of your potential customers, and your customer base will stop engaging with you.

Marketing is not a one-time fix, it's an ongoing process just like any other. Would you go to the gym for six months and call it good for your lifetime fitness journey? No way. If you have goals and want to see results, you have to commit to something you do every day to get the results you desire.

Many people stopped marketing in 2020 during the pandemic because they were uncertain of the times ahead. What a lot of people don't realize, however, is that this is actually the best time to advertise. When the number of competitors dips, there's an opportunity. In fact, during the pandemic people were online more than ever as they worked from home. Rates were cheap. We all knew COVID-19 wouldn't last forever and whoever pressed on during these times came out on top. People were still buying, they were just buying differently.

I'm always amazed when I meet with clients who have spent years going off of only referrals for their lead generation. Don't get me wrong, referrals from happy clients are the best leads, but you'll always stay within your circle of influence if you don't market outside of your circle too. It's really hard to create a growing, successful business if you don't try to broaden your clientele through advertising. We've been privileged to work with clients from Fiji, Canada, and Australia through our marketing efforts. These people would never know about D2 Branding if we hadn't done a marketing campaign outside the realm of client referrals.

The key is finding marketing that works the best for your audience. You have to have the right message for the right people - an irresistible offer to get them to react.

People ask me all the time what the best marketing strategies are. The truth is, it completely depends on the audience you're going after and where they spend their time. Is it business to business? Then LinkedIn is a great option for you. Do you have a health-related product or women's clothing brand? Then Facebook, Instagram and TikTok are great options for you. Are you trying to reach senior citizens? We've had success with Facebook ads and ads in print magazines tailored to that niche audience. The best thing to do is have a marketing expert evaluate your audience, your messaging, and your irresistible offer and come up with a plan that fits within your budget. The most important thing to do is track your return on investment. You should be making more money than you're spending on marketing, and once you see the return, you increase your ad spending to increase that return. And guess what? The cycle never, ever stops.

Now that you've mastered marketing and know it takes the entire marketing mix to succeed, it's time to make some money!

Want to Control Your Destiny? Make Money and Learn What to Do With It!

Now that you've learned how to market, you have to master sales. This is one of my favorite topics because sales can control your destiny! Entrepreneurs who know how to sell, end up on top. You don't want to waste your marketing dollars getting good leads that don't turn into sales.

Can you think of a time in your life when money played a factor in an important decision you made? Or, maybe you couldn't make the right decision because you didn't have the money to do so?

My mom got pregnant with my older brother while she was still in high school. Because my dad's family was Catholic and lived in a small town in Kansas where having a baby out of wedlock was unheard of, the two had to quickly get married.

My sweet mom raised three kids and sacrificed all of her dreams to be a mom. Before she turned 40, however, she and my dad divorced. My mom was scared because she had never been on her own and never had a job. With that support gone, she found herself with no degree or work experience – a single mom of three kids needing to get a job. That was a scary time for her.

During this time, I saw money dictate her life decisions. I was in 7th grade at the time and vowed I would never rely on anyone for money. Instead, I would be self-sufficient, and if I needed to pack up my kids and move somewhere to have a better life, I would do it. By the grace of God, my mom went on to get an administrative job with State Farm Insurance in their regional office and worked her way up to a managerial role through hard work and dedication.

I recently read a quote that reminded me of this part of my story: "Money, or the lack thereof, will put you at the mercy of someone else."

When you don't have your own money, you're at the mercy of whoever is paying you. If you work for a boss, they dictate how much money you make and how often you work – it's not up to you, unless you're commission-based. If you're a stay-at-home mom, more often than not, your husband will dictate how much money you spend. That idea never sat well with me. Once I started making my own money, I felt like I was way more in control of my destiny and could make the best decisions for me and my family.

If you're a business owner with one or two clients who make up the majority of your revenue, you might find yourself in a tough spot down the road. It's so exciting to get a new high-paying client, but what happens if that client backs out and all of your resources are dedicated to them? If you're not diversified with your revenue, that big client will control you, and you'll be at their mercy.

We have a diversified client base at D2 Branding now, but we didn't start that way. Having a diverse client base allows us to make smart business decisions, like letting a client go, if needed. It's never fun to 'fire' a client, but sometimes it's necessary, and if you're too tied to them financially, you won't have the freedom to do so.

The same principle applies to your team. If one person has all of the expertise in one area, they are harder to replace. You need to have good systems and processes in place so in the event one team member leaves, it's easy to train a new hire.

Accounting was the most difficult thing for me to handle at the launch of my business. I was good at making money but I wasn't great at managing it. That is why my first hire was an accountant.

What if I'm Scared to Sell? Five Ways to Overcome Fear in Sales

It's totally normal to be scared to sell. It can be intimidating to put yourself out there and risk being rejected. That being said, overcoming this fear is essential to growing as an entrepreneur and taking your business to the next level. That's why I put together this list of the five ways you can start to get over your fear in sales so you can hit your revenue goals!

1. Figure out the source of your fear!

Ask yourself:

- Are you scared of rejection?
- Are you not confident in the product or service you are selling?
- Are you worried about coming across as too pushy?

The reality is, we all face rejection in sales. We have to accept that not every sale we try to make will close. In fact, research shows that, on average, people will close only 10 percent of the time when cold-calling (this means that you're trying to sell to a 'cold' market, not a 'warm' market that's already familiar with you). A potential client or customer will have to go from cold, to warm, to hot, in order to buy. A cold market has never heard of you and is not familiar with what you are selling. A warm market is getting to know you, but hasn't put their trust in you yet. A hot market knows you, likes you and trusts you enough to buy!

In the beginning, all of your prospects will be considered a cold market, unless you're selling to your friends and family. That's why your circle of influence is a great place to start in sales. If there's a group of people in your life that you have established relationships with who are also your ideal and likely buyers, start with them. As you get more comfortable with your pitch, you can expand into a colder market with people you don't know yet.

2. Confront your fear head-on.

The only way to overcome fear is to confront it head-on. Trust me when I say that everyone is fearful to some degree when starting sales calls. And odds are, you won't land a sale on your first (or even 10th) call, but you have to keep trying until you hit.

I highly recommend scripting out your pitch and practicing and rehearsing it over and over in the mirror, or videoing yourself, until you get comfortable saying it. Not only will doing this remove some of the fear and discomfort you may feel during a sales call, but it will also help you sound much more natural and relaxed to your potential client or customer. You don't want to sound like you are using a script on your calls, but you have to start somewhere until you get it down. Bottom line, practice makes perfect, and you'll never reach your goals until you dive in and get started.

The best thing I learned years ago is to not take it personally when someone doesn't buy, even if they're your friend. Your product or service is not for everyone, which is why defining your niche market is so important. If you're solving a problem for your niche market, they will buy. Who cares if you get rejected? Don't sweat it. Just evaluate what you could do better and then move on to the next potential client. And just because they said, no thanks initially, doesn't mean it's a completely closed door. I've had many people come back to me six months or a year after I pitched to them, ready to buy.

3. Don't sell anything you aren't confident in.

Over the years, I've made the mistake of trying to sell someone else's product or service that I just didn't believe in. What I found is that I wasn't nearly as successful as I was selling my own services that I knew I could deliver on. What it comes down to is truly believing in what you have to offer, before anyone else will.

I recommend writing down all of the great things about your product or service and looking it over before every sales call. I also recommend memorizing one or two success stories of happy customers that you can share with your potential customer. Stories sell better than scripts every time, because they're authentic and genuine, and they help you build a connection with your customer. If you tell your potential customer a story about a customer just like them who had success, they will take notice.

4. Sell with your own style.

Everyone has a different sales style. I've watched very confident salespeople who come across as pushy and almost make the customer feel dumb if they don't buy, but it works for them. Don't get me wrong - you definitely don't want the customer to feel dumb - but if you make it so obvious that your product or service is what they have to have to solve their problem, they come to the conclusion it's a no-brainer to buy.

I've also seen other, more casual sales reps, who have a gift of building ridiculous rapport with their potential clients. They become friends with them before they even sell anything. This approach can also be very successful! The best approach is YOU being YOU!

My advice is to follow best sales practices, but tailor them to your personal comfort zone. You'll feel more confident selling when you can be you. Remember that the best salespeople are also the best listeners. Nothing is worse than selling to someone who doesn't want what you're selling, and you won't know this until you start asking questions. My best piece of wisdom in sales is to always be yourself. You will come across much more genuine than someone who's following someone else's script.

5. Selling is serving!

You have to approach sales by looking at it as if you are serving the person on the other side. You have something great to offer them that can genuinely improve their lives or their businesses. Once you have the confidence that you're doing your potential customer a favor by presenting them with your offer, sales will seem like a breeze!

Once you have all of this down, it's time to go for it! When I first started selling for 918moms.com, I didn't know what I was doing. We were just starting out, so we didn't have much traffic on our site yet. What it took was me walking into businesses over and over to perfect my pitch and get truly comfortable with it. Then I started to observe which parts of my pitch piqued interest in potential buyers. I started to tailor and craft my message based on the responses I got until it worked most of the time! Practice makes perfect. Remember, you have to call on 100 people on average, to get 10 yeses. That's 90 no's! The quicker you get through the list, the quicker you will get to the yeses!

Mastering the Sales Call

Do you ever end a sales call and think, "Why did I say that?" I've personally done that many times, but I value each pitch as an opportunity to learn.

In business, you're always selling something. If you're an employee, you're selling your skills or expertise to a company. If you're a freelancer, you're selling professional services to clients. If you're an entrepreneur, you're selling yourself to investors, joint venture partners or potential clients. If you can sell in business, then you will be successful. If you can't sell, don't worry – it's a skill you can learn!

There are small things you can do on a sales call to sound more confident and get more sales. Confidence is key – no one wants to buy from someone who is unsure of their product or service. You never want to sound desperate, like you need to get the sale to survive. You must have the mindset that you have something this client needs, and you're the solution to their biggest problem. Showing certainty in yourself and in the product or service you're selling is absolutely essential. In all my years in sales, I've found that confidence matters more than competence because confident people always get the sale.

Tony Robbins puts it this way: Success – in life and in business – is 80% mindset and 20% skill. So, let's get your mindset right!

I've made hundreds of sales calls throughout my career, so I came up with a list of my top "Instead of this, try this" sales call tips.

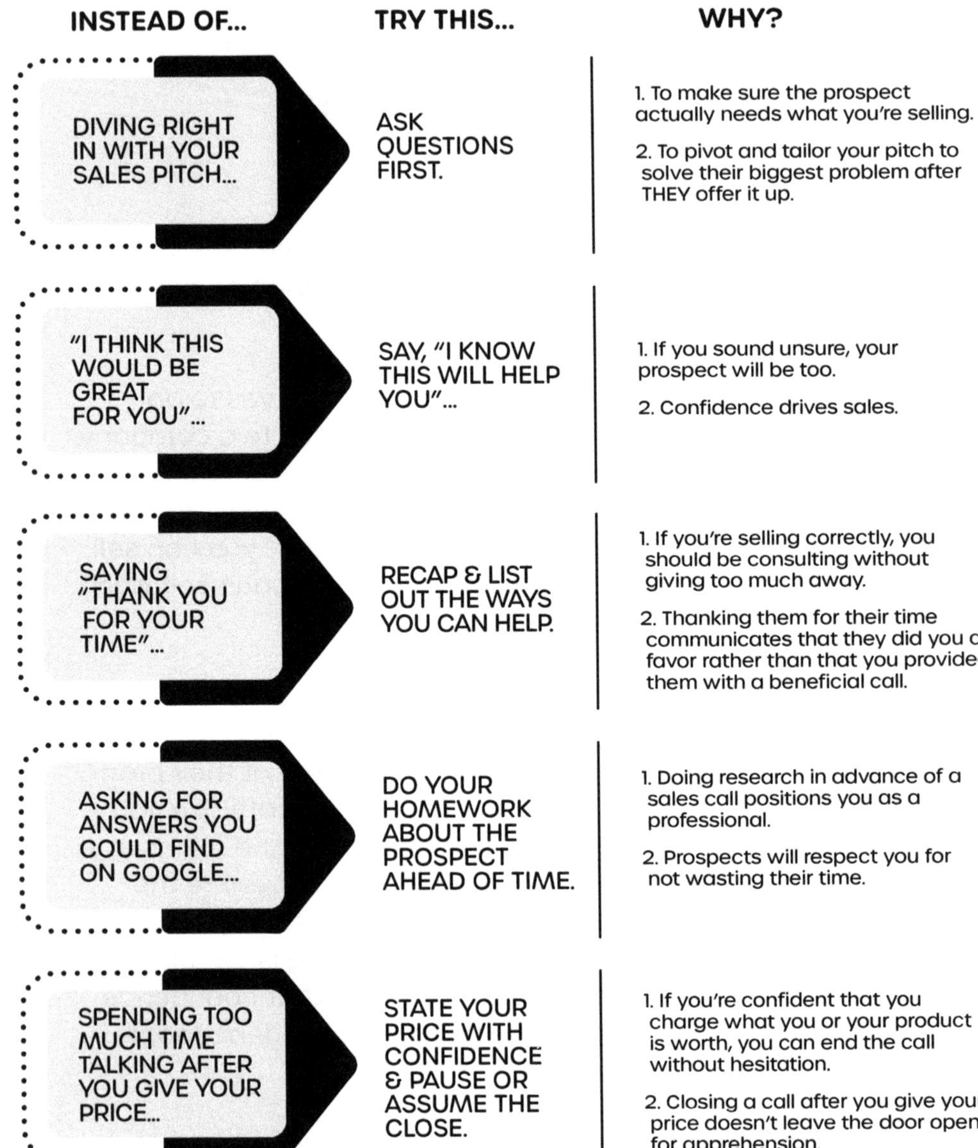

INSTEAD OF...	TRY THIS...	WHY?
DIVING RIGHT IN WITH YOUR SALES PITCH...	ASK QUESTIONS FIRST.	1. To make sure the prospect actually needs what you're selling. 2. To pivot and tailor your pitch to solve their biggest problem after THEY offer it up.
"I THINK THIS WOULD BE GREAT FOR YOU"...	SAY, "I KNOW THIS WILL HELP YOU"...	1. If you sound unsure, your prospect will be too. 2. Confidence drives sales.
SAYING "THANK YOU FOR YOUR TIME"...	RECAP & LIST OUT THE WAYS YOU CAN HELP.	1. If you're selling correctly, you should be consulting without giving too much away. 2. Thanking them for their time communicates that they did you a favor rather than that you provided them with a beneficial call.
ASKING FOR ANSWERS YOU COULD FIND ON GOOGLE...	DO YOUR HOMEWORK ABOUT THE PROSPECT AHEAD OF TIME.	1. Doing research in advance of a sales call positions you as a professional. 2. Prospects will respect you for not wasting their time.
SPENDING TOO MUCH TIME TALKING AFTER YOU GIVE YOUR PRICE...	STATE YOUR PRICE WITH CONFIDENCE & PAUSE OR ASSUME THE CLOSE.	1. If you're confident that you charge what you or your product is worth, you can end the call without hesitation. 2. Closing a call after you give your price doesn't leave the door open for apprehension.

Sales calls take practice, but once you're comfortable, you'll be amazed at how easily your sales will close. Start by cleaning up any of the mistakes I outlined above to set yourself up for sales success!

Customers Buy for Pain or Pleasure

There are two things you can offer people to make them buy your product or service: getting them out of pain, or bringing them pleasure.

First, let's talk about pain. Think of the weight loss industry – they play off of pain. It's painful to feel unhealthy and not love the way you look and feel. The weight loss industry takes this pain and uses it to promise consumers a new life; one full of happiness and newfound joy. They replace a deep pain point for consumers with pleasure.

To use a personal example, marketing can often be painful for our clients at D2 Branding. They try to handle their own marketing, but they don't know the best practices, how much they should spend on ads, or what platforms to use to reach their ideal customers. This process can be painful for them and not very rewarding. That's why we market ourselves as being the solution to their marketing problems. If you solve peoples' problems, they will buy from you.

When you're putting together your marketing copy or your sales presentation, make a list of the reasons people will buy from you. Are you alleviating their pain, bringing them pleasure, or both? What problems in your target audience's world can you solve? That's your pitch!

It's worth noting that you don't want to get too into the weeds sharing every detail of your process. For example, if I'm selling a search engine optimization (SEO) package, I tell my client that we'll get them to the top of Google for key terms in their industry and once they're there, they'll start to get calls. I don't get into all the technical details of how SEO works, because they don't need to know them. They just need to trust that we can deliver on our promise. Instead of breaking down our lengthy process for each client, we showcase case studies and testimonials on our website that show how we've helped past clients accomplish similar goals.

Once I worked with a lawn company who specialized in pest control. They were giving way too many details in their sales process and it cost them sales. Customers looking for a lawn company want to know that you are trustworthy, have a credible track record and will get rid of their weeds! Occasionally, someone may ask more technical questions, and when that happens, always answer them. But avoid starting with too much information, or you risk losing attention.

Start with a hook to get people interested, then throw in a story of how you've helped a real customer just like them, and end with an offer they can't refuse.

Using the lawn company example:

> Hook: "What if I told you we could get rid of all your weeds in just 30 days, and you'll have the best-looking lawn on the block?" This hook should grab their attention and make them want to learn more.
>
> Story: "We just finished up weed control for a house in this area that had more weeds than you. After 30 days, everything in their yard looks healthy and bright green." This story should be something real that your business has accomplished to help you establish credibility. Photo evidence is always helpful!

Offer: "If you sign up this week, your first spray, valued at____ dollars, is free!" An offer should be a reason to buy right now.

The hook, story and offer strategy is a tried and true method to making sales.

When you're on a sales call, the quicker you can address your customer's pain, the better. People are busier now than ever and don't have time to sit on the phone for an hour. Greet them, establish rapport, and then start qualifying them as a potential client by asking questions. The more you listen, the more you can tailor your message to meet their needs.

When I'm on sales calls for D2 Branding, I usually ask, "What is the biggest thing that keeps you up at night when it comes to your marketing?" This question helps me learn what their pain points are, and what I can do to take their stress away. Then, I ask what success in marketing looks like to them. From there, I can tailor our services to meet their exact needs while also sharing with them our X-Factor (the things that make us different from any other agency).

Your Sales Plan

Now that you know the "why" behind sales, what not to say on a sales call, and how important selling is to grow your business, it's time to block out time in your week to generate sales. When most entrepreneurs start their businesses, they end up being the sales person because they can't afford to hire anyone right away. I can promise you, though, that you'll never regret hiring a good sales person! Here are the steps you need to take to get started:

1. Block off at least two hours every day to cold call. This could be calling on potential customers or referral partners that could send business your way.

2. Create a Dream 100 list of potential buyers. You won't be productive in sales unless you have a list to go off of. Get your list organized so when you sit down for two hours per day, you are ready to call. For example, I go after female CEOs and entrepreneurs for potential coaching clients. One of the easiest ways to find these prospects is through LinkedIn. If you have LinkedIn Navigator, you can pull very detailed lists. Let's just say I wanted to go after CEOs of companies with 100+ employees that were graduates of Oklahoma State University. I could do it! LinkedIn has gotten more crowded and it is harder to break through the noise with all of the messaging, but many of these prospects have their business emails listed on their profile, so you can email them as well. You know the name of their company, so with one phone call

to the company, you can find out their direct line or their assistant's name and direct line. Now you have a great prospect to reach out to. Remember, you have to have a HOOK to get people interested in talking to you, just like when you run an ad—something that stops them in their tracks. You have to hook them with something that hits a pain point for them. I might say something like, "Are you tired of not being in control of your destiny and being chained to your desk all day every day? What if you could call the shots and work the hours you want to work while making the money you want to make working from anywhere in the world?" Then I share a quick story from my experience of creating a personal brand and becoming an entrepreneur or a story from one of my client's who have achieved what they want, which is usually time freedom to work whenever they want and financial freedom to make as much money as they desire. Then I offer a free 30 minute evaluation of their personal brand, which is my consultative sales pitch. This is a way of sharing your knowledge to help them and also sharing your product or service. Maybe they are on LinkedIn and post some about their business but they haven't been strategic in creating a personal brand that they could get paid for. Most people will listen to a free evaluation, especially if it is specifically about them. That's my "hook, story and offer." If I went right in and said, "I have a six-month coaching program that costs $20,000 up front," they would think I was crazy. I have to establish rapport, give them VALUE so they start to get to know me, like me, and trust me. I have to hit on all of the pain points...those things that keep them up at night (maybe it's missing out on their kid's events because they are always traveling for work or are too busy to break away). I know these pain points because I had them too when I worked in corporate America. I can relate to them, empathize with them, and share my story with them. Some of my favorite coaching clients have come from LinkedIn. They did my six-month coaching program and are still coaching with me today, years later.

3. Once you have your list, it's time to reach out. This means calling, texting, emailing—offering VALUE! Selling something like a $20,000 coaching package isn't something you usually sell in that first 30-minute free consultation. It takes weeks or even months sometimes to get people to buy big ticket items. You have to nurture your leads until they are ready to take the leap. If you are sending them emails offering value, there could come a day where they are really fed up at the office or with their boss, and they will reach out. You want potential clients or customers to think of you first. They're ready to buy when their pain is deep enough that they are ready for a solution to their problem! If you do not have a CRM to keep track of this list, use a Google Sheet or Excel spreadsheet. I've always just kept my leads on a Google Sheet that I update and review daily. I have the prospect's name, company name, phone number, email, website address and detailed notes of our conversation, so I can look back and know exactly what we talked about at the time. The other day I followed up with a woman who had been tending to her mother-in-law in hospice when I first reached out. We had a great conversation, but obviously she was not in any mental capacity to think about starting a personal brand or adding anything to her schedule. I pivoted and just did a coaching session with her about how she had to focus on controlling the things she could control and free up time in her day to care for her loved one and take care of herself. She was grateful for the call. When we got off the phone, I put a note in my calendar to follow up with her in six months. Six months came around, and I left a voicemail telling her I was thinking about her and hoped everything was going well in her life and that I was available if she wanted to talk. Sure enough, she called me back and her mother-in-law had passed and she was in the mental state to talk about her personal branding business. I haven't closed the sale yet, but I shared all of the information with her and painted a picture

of what her life could be like once she created a personal brand. If anything, I know I touched her life and opened her eyes to new possibilities, which is my ultimate goal.

4. Color code your list so you can look at it and quickly know who you need to follow up with first. I like to make the closed leads green, the ones that say no in red and the ones I have pitched but not closed yet in yellow. The ones that are white or not color coded yet are ones I have reached out to but haven't been able to reach. So, if I only have 30 minutes in my day, I quickly go to the "yellows" which are warm leads and start following up! I have reached out to people 15 times before I closed them! Stay relentless and stick with it. Remember, you aren't a used car salesman, you are offering value! People don't mind this if you are genuinely helping them out, offering advice, and showing them how you can solve their biggest problem. Don't get me wrong, I've had plenty of people hang up on me or tell me no, but it doesn't phase me. It wasn't the right time in their life, so I move on to the next. The quicker I get through the no's the quicker I get to the YESES!

5. You need to have multiple ways of obtaining leads, not just through cold calling. Ideally, you will have leads coming from Google, leads coming from a digital Facebook + Instagram + TikTok + LinkedIn ad campaign, as well as regular referrals that come your way from happy clients and referral partners. Once you have all of these lead generation systems in place, you are on your way to getting sales! Remember, on average it takes 100 calls to close 10, so don't be discouraged when you start hearing "no." Instead, look at it as "not right now," but there will probably be a time in their future when it does make sense. Thank them for their time and move on to the next prospect. Keep the "not right now," on your email list where you can continue to add VALUE to keep them engaged and reach out to them every few months or so

to see how things are going. I do this all of the time and usually have one or two that are interested at a later date. They are always surprised that I remembered our conversation and am following up.

To recap: here are your action steps:

1. Plan when you are going to do sales each day and block off your schedule.

2. Create a Dream 100 sales list of potential prospects to call on.

3. Call, text, and email, offering VALUE.

4. Keep diligent notes on your actions, and color code prospects based on interest level.

5. Set up a plan to generate leads through cold calling, referrals, Google ads, and digital ads.

Five Things I Wish I Would Have Done at the Launch of My Business

Now that we've touched on how to build your personal brand, create your marketing plan, and start selling, it's time to talk about building your business. I know most people like to build the business out first, and then start to market and make money, but I do the opposite.

I advise you to start marketing and making money on the one thing you are great at and build the business systems and processes along the way. It's much easier to do this with some revenue coming in. At D2 Branding, I started selling business coaching right away because it only required my time and I didn't need a team to start. I just needed my laptop and my coaching plan. Believe me, it wasn't smooth sailing all of the time—we definitely had growing pains. I didn't have a coach to guide me along the way in the beginning, so it was a lot of trial and error until we started to get our systems and processes in place to be able to scale.

It's easy to look back with the benefit of hindsight and wish you would've done things differently – especially when it comes to business!

Being a business coach now, there are so many things I wish I would've known from day one. Here are the top five things I wish I would've done when I first launched my business.

Hire faster. When I first started my business, my team only consisted of myself and an assistant, so I was very limited when it came to how many clients I could take on. This situation led to me turning many clients away. Looking back, I can't imagine how many thousands of dollars I turned away! Now, I coach people to scale their team as their business scales so that they don't end up turning away money. When there's a demand for your product or service and you can't meet it, you have to make a choice: hire more people or stay stagnant. If you're sure that the business is there, it makes sense to expand and make money off of that demand. I operate off of this principle now – I hire as soon as I see a need and I don't hesitate.

Create an SEO strategy on day one. At the beginning of my business, I offered SEO services to clients, but I didn't optimize our own website for Google. We had plenty of referrals coming in, but what about all of those people searching Google for exactly what we have to offer, but have no idea who we are as a company? Now, we come to the top of Google for many key terms in our industry and we close clients all of the time because of that. The challenge, however, with putting money into an SEO strategy is that you won't see a return right away. You have to slowly work your way to the top of Google in order to get leads coming in. It's a long game, but when you're at the top of Google, you'll get calls and leads from Google that are much more qualified, because they are already searching for what you have! I would start SEO on day one.

Charge for marketing plans. I can't even tell you how many hours I spent helping people create full-blown marketing plans for free. The goal was to share my skills, knowledge and expertise to gain their trust so they would hire D2 to handle their marketing. Many people did hire us, but some of them didn't because they either thought our services were too expensive or they already had the knowledge that I'd given them, for free. I regretted spending hours coaching them instead of selling them our services. I gave them the game plan they needed without even charging them. Now, I only book paid coaching sessions with clients because I realize how much money my knowledge is worth. This process has added an additional revenue stream for D2, and it's also become one of my favorite things to do. Remember, you are the expert. Your skills, knowledge and expertise are worth money. Just like you pay an expert to cut your hair, decorate your house, and teach your children, you are an expert who should be paid for your time and advice.

Build a list. I often think back on all of the people I've crossed paths with over the years whose information I forgot to gather. In the last five years, I started gathering peoples' contact information for a list so I can remarket to them with email marketing, text marketing or phone calls to get their business. There have been many times when I've checked in with potential clients I first met years ago, to see how it's going. Some of them couldn't afford D2 services or my coaching at the time we initially connected, but now, their business is ready to go to the next level. I use my list to keep diligent notes on all past potential clients, so I can have great conversations with them in my follow-up calls and not just sound like I'm trying to sell them something.

Every time I go to the dentist, my hygienist asks me something specific related to what we talked about six months prior, at my last appointment. I'm always so impressed at how she remembers specific things, so I asked her about it one day. She said that she doesn't actually remember all of it, but right when a patient leaves, she goes to the computer and writes down notes next to their name so she can remember specifics about them for next time. I couldn't stop thinking about this amazing customer service tip and I couldn't wait to implement it into my own business and life. The only way to control the leads that come to you and convert them into sales is to build a list and nurture it! I now have thousands of people on a list, but I might have had 100,000 if I'd started day one.

Create a front-end offer. This offer is a hook to get your potential customer in, followed by a back-end offer to upsell clients. This strategy is something I recently created for our business. We have a lot of clients on the marketing side of things come to us because they need a web presence – a new website, an upgrade for their existing website or Google optimization. I realized I had leads coming in from a variety of different services we offer at D2, but we didn't have a funnel in place to take a client from one of our services and upgrade them to another.

Now, we have a sales funnel that approaches businesses with a proposal to improve their websites and get them more leads online. This offer is a good hook to get them introduced to D2 and show them the other services we offer so we can become their go-to agency for all things creative and lead generation-related.

You need a plan to get leads, nurture them, close them and upsell them. I spent many years just taking whatever clients came my way rather than strategically planning who I was going after, offering them a hook, closing them and upselling them on additional services.

Here's how you can create a plan like this:

1. Decide which audience you want to go after. Remember, if you market to everyone, no one will respond. There are riches in niches.

2. Create a hook to get your clients interested. Maybe your hook can be a free ebook with great information from your industry that solves a problem for them. This is your front-end offer.

3. Capture the names, phone numbers and emails of your potential clients so you can nurture those leads.

4. Allow them to get to know you, like you, and trust you, then close the lead.

5. Upsell them your back-end offer.

Create a plan and stick to it – you will see results.

Until I hired a business coach of my own, I didn't know the necessary steps I needed to take to build and scale. Now, I have a clear plan with goals I'm trying to reach and systems and processes in place to get me there.

Something as easy as keeping every single lead that comes my way on a Google sheet with their name, contact information, how they found me and what their needs are, is a simple thing I do to be proactive for my business. This list is gold because it's composed of leads who already know me and trust me, I just have to nurture them until they buy. Circumstances change, budgets change and frustration sets in. My job is to stay relevant in leads' minds so when they are ready for the next step, they think of D2.

If you're a new business owner, don't make the same mistakes I did. Hire as quickly as it makes sense for your business, create an SEO strategy, charge for your knowledge, build a list, and create a front-end offer as soon as you can.

Why Do Smart Women Make Financial Mistakes?

Once you start making money, you have to figure out what to do with it. As you can tell by now, accounting has never been my thing. I would much rather spend money than save money, and I like to reward myself for my hard work. I've never had a poverty mindset in my life because I know I can always make more money. But as my business has grown and scaled, I've had to learn how to control my finances, business expenses and payroll.

I tried to do my own accounting for many years, but I constantly made mistakes. I didn't trust anyone else but myself to handle my accounting, which didn't make sense because math had never been my thing in the first place! By attempting to do my own accounting and continually making avoidable errors, I was actually hurting my bottom line, not helping it.

As D2 Branding continued to grow and make more money, I knew it was time for me to seek the help of a financial expert who could assist me with accounting and budgeting instead of trying to do it myself. It was such a relief to pass off my accounting needs, investments and retirement fund to a trusted financial advisor who could guide me in the right direction. I don't have to think about what to do with my money anymore, I just need to make the money, and he advises me what I should do with it. With the help of a financial advisor, I have a better understanding of where my money is, how much I'm making, how much I can take home, and how much I need to save than I ever had before.

The financial aspect of my business is probably the area I've made the most mistakes in along the way —mostly small, unintentional errors with money that can be detrimental if you don't come up with the right solution. My biggest accounting mistake was when I first started using Stripe, which is a great payment processing platform. I had one of my largest paying clients add TikTok ads as a service to their marketing, so my assistant put them into the system to be charged $4,000/ month. A few weeks later, they called to tell me they were going to wait on this service but I forgot to tell my assistant because I wasn't used to using the new system. Meanwhile 14 months go by before we discover the mistake and we have been charging them $4,000 additional per month, which was $56,000! I was so mortified, I called the client right away and told them what happened. I even cried to them, which I NEVER do. I think I cry every two years at the most, so this shows you the level of stress I had at the time. The client was extremely understanding, which they did not have to be, whatsoever. The lessons I learned from this were to always be honest and come clean immediately. I did not have a good excuse. I just told them it was my mistake and of course I paid them back. I also learned it was time to pay someone that was a professional accountant! This was a costly mistake that could have cost me one of my largest paying clients!

Many of the entrepreneurs I work with struggle with their finances as well. I talk to entrepreneurs who have no idea how much money they should be taking home or if they can afford to hire someone to work under them, which can prevent them from scaling up their business.

After reflecting on my own struggles with finances, I came up with the six most common mistakes I see entrepreneurs make with money.

1. Hiring in advance of revenue

When you first start your business, chances are you'll need to suck it up and do all of the work – even the things you don't like to do – until you bring in enough revenue to hire someone. In my experience, it's not a good idea to go into debt before you launch. Unless you have an expensive buildout (like a brick and mortar storefront), it may not be necessary to hire people before you launch. That's the reason why I coach people to create online businesses – you'll have no overhead costs as you try to get your business off the ground.

In my opinion, it's better to start making some money and then hire your first employee. Once you start getting some sales, you can hire a virtual assistant who you pay by the hour or an accountant who helps you navigate your finances. Until the money starts rolling in, you'll be doing all of that work yourself, but think of it this way: You'll have no problem training the person you eventually hire because you've been in the trenches, doing the work for yourself.

2. Borrowing money when you don't really need it, but when the bank is willing to lend it.

If you don't need to take out a loan, borrow money, or get an investor, don't do it. It will only add extra pressure and stress. If you can go without a paycheck for a while, do it – that's what many bootstrapping entrepreneurs have to do when they're first starting out. Taking out a massive loan to pay yourself $100,000 a year isn't a good idea. Start making money first, then pay yourself. Make sure not to borrow unless you absolutely need to to pay for your operations in the beginning.

3. Not paying payroll taxes on time.

Pay your taxes, period! I didn't pay quarterly taxes during my first year of working as an entrepreneur, and it was brutal. I owed almost $40,000 at the end of the year because I didn't plan ahead. We had to take money out of my husband's $401k and suffered major penalties because of it. I learned from this experience and hired an accountant who helped me set money aside each month to pay for quarterly taxes, which made it much more manageable.

If you get behind on your taxes, the IRS will come knocking at your door and you could go to jail. Stay up-to-date on your taxes and enlist the help of a professional – you won't regret it!

4. Pricing your products or services too low.

Charge what you are worth! I was coaching an amazing entrepreneur who sold a weight loss product online for $7.77 a month. I was shocked – you can barely get one Starbucks drink for that price! People weren't taking her seriously because the low price made her program seem less valuable. After I met with her, we decided to start charging $777 a month, and then she started to get sales. She was able to scale her business up and hire additional employees to help her grow the company.

If your pricing is too low, there's a preconceived notion that your product or service must not be very good. Being the cheapest option is not always the best idea. Don't focus on being the cheapest, focus on being the best. When you have an undeniably awesome product, the price won't matter.

5. Permitting accounts receivable.

Don't permit accounts receivables. What I mean is the practice of allowing people to owe you outstanding money. It's just not worth it. When I first started my business, I had four clients who owed me money and it added up to almost $20,000. I spent so much extra time hounding them to pay me because I had already paid my employees and freelancers for their work, and in the end, I ended up never getting paid back for some of the services we provided. After that experience, I knew my model needed to change.

Moving forward, I only took payments up front for services. I had my clients' credit cards on file that I charged with automatic monthly payments. This way, I never have to talk to the client about payment unless their card didn't go through. If a card declines at the beginning of the month, we don't do any work until we're paid. Now, I have no accounts receivables and it's been such a huge weight lifted. I'm firm about this policy, and my clients respect it.

6. Relying on one major source of revenue.
You should never put yourself in the position of having just one revenue source. You need to diversify your revenue in case one area takes a hit. For example, a few months ago Facebook and Instagram were down for hours. That's an entire day where all of my clients' ads didn't run. We both lost money, but luckily, I have other revenue streams, so it wasn't too detrimental overall. But what if one day, Facebook shuts down for a day, or a week or all together? We can't risk relying on something for all of our revenue that's completely out of our control. This is why we are diversified – business coaching, digital marketing, SEO, video production, photography, website design, graphic design and social media are all streams of income for the team at D2 Branding.

Money can determine the course of both your personal and professional life.

In your day-to-day life and in your business, financial independence allows you to make sound decisions and find success without being at the mercy of external factors. By following these six strategies to manage money effectively, you can take charge of your financial destiny and live the life you want to live!

Invest In You, In Your Business, In Marketing & In Sales

Investing is hard at the start of your business. I get it. When money is going out but not coming in, it can be extremely stressful. But, you have to invest in certain things in order to make money. No one starts off day one making money without putting money into their business. I've met with many entrepreneurs that spend thousands of dollars, some over a hundred thousand dollars, on their build out, their signage, their website but then they say they don't have any money to market. Why would you invest all of that money in your business and not put a plan in place to market it? Just because you have a website doesn't mean anyone will know to go to it! You will never regret investing in you as a leader, in your business, your marketing or a sales team!

Five Reasons You Must Invest In Your Business

As an entrepreneur, sometimes it can be hard to invest in your business but it will come to the point where you can only do so much by yourself. At the end of the day, the money you put into it, is the money that comes directly out of your pocket.

I once had a client who really needed to invest in a software to help them navigate their leads, kick off a marketing campaign, and hire another person. Taking these steps would cut into their take-home pay, but it was necessary for growth.

Sometimes, you have to take a step back in your revenue to take your business five steps forward.

I always encourage my clients to weigh the benefits of adding an additional expense. How much more business can they bring in if they hire a new person? Can they double the work they're producing by having another person there to share the load? How much potential revenue would that change bring in? The challenging part, however, is that sometimes you may not see the return on that investment for months or even years.

If you're making a change to your business – hiring someone new, starting a marketing campaign, buying new software – it's important to have a process in place to evaluate the return on your investment (ROI). The best way to do that is by creating a profit and loss statement and tracking the progress on it every month. This statement will show you how much money is going out and how much money is coming in, which will tell you if your new investments are working.

Investing in your business is incredibly important for many reasons. Mainly, it can provide a means for your company to innovate, develop and grow. Some investments I've made in D2 Branding haven't produced a return, but every one has helped us learn something valuable.

Here are five reasons why you must invest in your business:

1. **If you invest, you will grow.**
   You can't make more money if you don't invest in your business. Similarly, your bottom line can't increase if you don't offer additional products/services or hire additional staff. As an entrepreneur, there comes a point where you can't do everything yourself. You have to start outsourcing or hiring in order to get the job done. Whether you're investing in products to help you run your business more smoothly, hiring a business coach or outsourcing tasks, spending the money is worth it. Once I invested in hiring more people, I was able to offer more

marketing services so my revenue increased. You can't do it all at once, but invest where you can make the biggest return first.

2. Investing can help alleviate stress.
If you're doing everything in your business right now and find yourself working 12-hour days just to get it all done, you will burn out. Once you start to delegate and invest in people and new processes, your life will get simpler. You need to give yourself time for self-care or you will become overworked, which could lead to loss of passion for the work you're doing. Once I hired my first team member, my assistant, life got so much easier! She handled all of the little tasks that bogged me down, like taking over my calendar. That little transition allowed me to free up time to service current clients and sell to potential clients!

3. Investing legitimizes your business.
Once you start to invest in your business, you start to take it seriously and things feel much more real. You will work harder to get a return if you've put money into something. Once I hired a business coach and was paying $2,000 per month for a call once a week, I started to take the business more seriously. I blocked out time each week to work on the areas he told me to and I started to see progress. If I was getting free advice from him, I wouldn't have taken it as seriously but it was taking a good amount of money out of my pay, so I had a sense of urgency to grow.

4. Investing allows you to operate in your genius.
One of the benefits of investing in your business is that you give yourself space to focus on what you're best at. There's no need to do things you don't excel at, and those things probably take you much longer to do than the things that are your strengths. If you invest in your company by outsourcing or hiring staff, your first hire

should be someone who excels in what you're worst at. For me, this hire was an accountant. Now, I only do a handful of things, the things I like to do and the things that bring in revenue. I am either coaching a client, selling a new client, or working on my podcast. I have a team that fulfills all of the services we offer and I am no longer the first contact person. Once I delegated those duties to my team, my life became more peaceful and profitable. Your goal should be to do only the things you are a genius at and leave the rest to your team.

5. **Investing will save you time and money in the long run.** If your business processes aren't optimized, chances are you're spending too much time doing things that could be automated. Investing in your company allows you to spend more time on things that bring in revenue, like sales. You will end up saving time and money in the long run!

I encourage you to make it a priority to invest in your business. You don't have to do everything at once, but take a step back, look at what's working and what isn't and decide what to invest in first. You won't regret investing in your business. If anything, you'll probably regret not doing it sooner.

Six Ways to Grow Your Business

Now is a great time to take a look at your expenses and the revenue coming in to see what's working for you and what you should pivot away from. Maybe there are people in your business who are no longer serving you or your goals. Or, maybe your advertising dollars aren't being spent in the best way.

I met with a client recently who closely tracked where all of their customers came from. They quickly realized that the $100k they spent on radio advertisements didn't get them any return. Not a single one of their customers last year learned about them by hearing a radio ad. Instead, they had 33% of customers come from Google searches, 23% from Facebook and Instagram, and 39% were unknown.

A few things stuck out to me after meeting with this client. The first, radio ads cost lots of money with no ROI. This company (and nearly any company, for that matter) would be better off putting money toward Google and SEO. It's always hard to stop doing a strategy you've done for years, but when it's no longer working, you have to pivot. Tracking your customers is the best way to find out what's working and what's not. What is working is what you do more of, what is not working, you stop.

If you want to see your business continue to grow this year, I came up with six business strategies I recommend implementing.

1. Have a growth mindset.

Too many people watch the news and get scared about the economy, which causes them to pull back on their marketing. What they should be doing instead is ramping up their marketing while the competition is sleeping. Cost to earn a customer goes down when companies are pulling back. Now is the time to get aggressive to get ahead of your competition.

2. Create multiple channels for lead generation.

Most people have one source of lead generation, but that's not enough. I recommend these three ways to get more leads:

- Prioritize advertising on Google, so when people search for your product or service, your business comes to the top.
- Implement a digital marketing campaign to go after your ideal audience. The biggest platforms are still Facebook, Instagram, LinkedIn and TikTok. Identify which platform your audience spends the most time on and prioritize it.
- Start a referral program. The best lead you can get is from a happy customer who refers friends and family your way.

3. Hire sales reps and appointment setters.

You'll only get so far if you are handling all the sales yourself. If you want to grow, it helps to have multiple people pursuing new leads, nurturing them and closing them. Even if you aren't ready for someone to take over the closing process, you can hire appointment setters. These people can tee up calls for you to close.

4. Have multiple front-end offers.

We talked about this earlier. What is your "offer" that brings people in? You should have a "hook" in place to get them through the door and then upsell them with backend offers. An example of this process in the marketing world would be to do a free website audit to get them in, share the information you gathered, then upsell them a new website based on your findings. This strategy is a great way to give them value with an audit and also make them realize they need something better.

5. Put real case studies on your website and share them on social media.

Testimonials are great, but if I can look at a real case study with a similar client, I'm sold. You should include information about where your client was before they started working with you, the strategy you used to improve their business, and the final results.

6. Find a coach who can guide you along the way.

Coaches can see things in your business that you can't see and can objectively tell you what needs to change. Every successful entrepreneur has a coach, a mentor or someone else on their team who holds them accountable and pushes them to greatness. I am a coach and I hire coaches! It always amazes me when a coach tells me something that I tell my clients all the time! How did I not think of it for my own business? It's because sometimes we're too close to it. Find someone who is where you want to be and hire them to link arms with you and guide you along the way! You'll never regret investing in a good coach!

Build a Team of Rockstars

Now that you've established your business, it's time for you to hire a team of rockstars!

One of the hardest things to do in business is build a team; a loyal tribe that would do anything for you and the business. Some of you might be thinking, is that even possible? Notice I don't call them employees, they are team members! Every member makes your company who it is and they are a direct reflection of you and your values. One of my favorite marketing gurus to follow, Gary Vee, posted this the other day and it caused controversy, "Your employees should not work as hard as you. It's not their business." Many of the entrepreneurs were offended by this thinking every team member should work as hard as them if they are getting paid. Trust me. Speaking from experience, this is not going to happen. No one will work as hard as you or care as much as you do. But if you create an amazing culture, they will go above and beyond in their work to serve clients. So how do you create a culture where people want to work every day and care about your clients or customers as much as you do?

Here are 5 ways I built a loyal tribe at D2 Branding:

1. Celebrate the Team!
You must celebrate your team! It is not about you it is about THEM! Make sure everyone on the team feels important and realizes their role is crucial as part of the whole! This is anyone and everyone because the entire

team must do their part for you to win! One of the most important things we have implemented, thanks to a business coach of mine, Alex Charfen, who runs the Billionaire Code, was to implement a daily huddle. Every morning from 8:45am-9am we all jump on a 15-minute Zoom call to go over our WINS from the day before and the "Big 3" things we are going to do that day to move the needle.

So many people get caught up in trying to do 25 things on their to-do list, and they feel like a failure at the end of the day when they haven't gotten through their entire list. We just focus on three things each team member can do today and that's it! Our daily huddle is also a time to connect with each other on a personal level and start our days off on positive notes! Many of our employees work remotely around the country, so it's a great way to connect before our days get busy with meetings. As a result of doing this, we have become closer as a team and our communication has greatly increased. Your team members want to feel valued and they want to feel like you care about them and the things going on in their personal lives. A daily huddle is an easy way to do this, one that I highly recommend!

2. Offer Perks!

One thing I always valued as an employee was a flexible work schedule, but I never got it. My first job working at an ad agency consisted of 12-hour days, Monday through Friday, and I still got paged on the weekends (yes I'm old enough to have had a pager...we didn't have cell phones yet). There was no regard for family time or time away from the office. I was essentially "on-call" 24 hours a day, seven days a week! It definitely taught me some serious work ethic, but also about balance. Luckily I was single then with no kids, because there's no way I could have managed being a mom and also working like that!

When I went on to work in television, I worked shorter days, but still 8:30am - 5:30pm every day. I would be the last one picking my kids up from daycare, getting there right before 6pm when they closed. My heart sank every time I saw my kids' sweet faces, tired from their own long days. That's when I knew if I ever had my own business, I would definitely have a flexible schedule for my team.

Some of the most efficient team members I have hired are moms! They are diligent in getting their work done because they know they need to get out of there and be a mom! When I hired my first employee, I decided we would work from 8:45am to 4pm Monday through Thursday with Fridays from home. That way we missed the traffic in the morning and at night and getting off at 4pm you still had time to run errands or go to your kid's events! I know what you are thinking: That's only a 7 hour day but I am paying them full time, 40 hours a week when in reality they are working 35. You are correct! We also implemented "work from home Fridays" and this was before COVID made it necessary to work from home. That way on a Friday, you could get your work accomplished while also throwing in a load of laundry or meeting a repairman at your house. Guess what happened? Production was great! The team put in their work and everyone was much happier workers! Yes, they work less than 40 hours a week, but productivity is at an all time high, so who really cares?

Flexibility is something that costs you nothing but can be a big component in creating a culture where people want to work! Team members will actually work harder for you and display loyalty from something as simple as flexibility! I still get to work at 7:30am every day and I often work on Fridays in the office, because that's my quiet time to plan, strategize and create my podcasts! But many Fridays I do some work in the morning and use the afternoon for errands I need to do so my weekends are free to be 100 percent present with my family. Flexibility is a great recruiting tool in hiring the right employees and keeping their loyalty for life!

3. Schedule Regular Check-Ins!

Sometimes your team members just want to be heard, kind of like your spouse. You may not have a solution for them, but more often than not, they just want you to listen. Schedule regular check-ins with your team so you can ask what's going great, what's keeping them from doing their job and any suggestions they have about how to improve the challenges they are facing. This will also give you a really good pulse on what's going on at the company.

I am the first to admit I get really busy in meetings all day and sometimes I'll forget to check in to see how the team is doing. I am very task-oriented and there are only so many hours in the day, so I have to remind myself to stop and check in to see how things are going. This is important! Many times the person at the top has no clue what's going on with the team members because they're too busy to ask!

This can be weekly meetings or even a quick smoothie run out of the office to connect. Nothing is more frustrating for a team member than feeling unheard.

4. Invest in Training!

If you are constantly improving your team's skills and knowledge and rewarding them financially for hitting milestones, they will remain loyal! We always try to ask if team members want to learn about another area of the business! Cross training will help when someone is sick or on vacation and you may find a superstar salesperson is stuck doing admin work! One way to assess the skills and personality of your team is to have them take the DISC profile test. I first saw this from Tony Robbins and was amazed how spot on it was for me when I took it. It has helped us in hiring and putting the right employees in the right positions based on their strengths. If you haven't ever taken a test like this, I encourage you to do it and have your staff do it as well! You may find someone is in the wrong position and will know why they are struggling! DISC stands for dominance, influence, compliance and steadiness.

I am sure this is not a shock to you but I am a high D, like off the charts...there's no middle of the road going on here! Here is the description of a high D:

The D Personality Style tends to be direct and decisive, sometimes described as dominant. They would prefer to lead than follow and tend towards leadership and management positions. They tend to have high self-confidence and are risk-takers and problem-solvers, enabling others to look to them for decisions and direction. They tend to be self-starters.

The good news:
Type D individuals think about big picture goals and tangible results. They are bottom-line organizers that can lead an entire group in one direction. They place great value on time frames and seeing results. The D may challenge the status quo and think in a very innovative way.

The bad news:
People with a D personality style tend to overstep authority, as they prefer to be in charge themselves. At times they can be argumentative and not listen to the reasoning of others. They tend to dislike repetition and routine and may ignore the details and minutia of a situation, even if it's important. They may attempt too much at one time, hoping to see quick results.

What is great about this is my assistant was the exact opposite of me on the spectrum. There's no way there could be two of me, it wouldn't work!

If you haven't tried it, it is fun to take! I am also a HUGE fan of the Enneagram test and I make all of my team and coaching clients take it. I am to the point now where I can usually tell what number someone is on the Enneagram after talking to them. With coaching clients, it helps me navigate how I coach them based on their personality type. I don't want to push too hard for someone that likes to stop and think and take a long time to make decisions or not push someone hard enough who is a doer!

5. Create a Team Environment

Create a team environment! Make sure everyone knows the company's core values and what you stand for, as well as your goals. If they know where you are going they can help you get there! Many leaders keep this all to themselves and then wonder why the team isn't working hard to achieve their goals. Maybe they don't even know there is a goal. They are just clocking in and clocking out each day doing their tasks without a championship to hustle for. We read our company tenants and core values at every staff meeting. We also share our "critical number," or scoreboard of where we are currently towards reaching our goal of 100 paying clients! Some companies use a revenue goal to go after, but we have found that the number of clients is something fun to track because most of our employees aren't commission-based. It is not as exciting for team members to track revenue if their pay is not based on revenue! Have a goal! Share it with the team! Celebrate the team when you get closer to your goal and go over the top when you achieve your goal! We also try to celebrate personal things in our team's lives like birthdays, getting married, having babies or even our kid's accomplishments! After all, many times we are with our work family more than we are with our real family, so treating them like family is a way to make them feel valued and loved and once you achieve this, their loyalty will be for life!

So if you want a team of ROCKSTARS, follow these 5 steps.

Why You Should Hire A Business Coach

People often ask me, "Why would I hire a business coach?," or, "When is the right time for me to hire a business coach?" My answer is always this: You can't afford NOT to have a business coach!

Most successful entrepreneurs have a business coach or a mentor who has helped them along the way. This is because it's impossible to be an expert in every area of your business, and an unbiased outside perspective can be very helpful when it comes to scaling your business and taking it to the next level.

Here are seven reasons why you should hire a business coach today!

1. Coaches can see what you can't see because they aren't emotionally attached to your business and don't work there every day. They can help you take a step back, see the bigger picture and be the visionary for your company.

2. Coaches help you focus and prioritize your business and your life. As entrepreneurs, we have a lot to juggle mentally, which can cause us to run around, going from meeting to meeting without a real plan in place. Coaches can help you map out your goals and create a plan of action to get you there.

3. A business coach can be a great source of accountability. As an entrepreneur, no one is holding you accountable to get things done because you're the boss. Having an external point of accountability in the form of a coach can be a powerful tool to keep you on track.

4. Coaches help you go further, faster. They have the blueprint to get you where you need to go because they've actually done the work and have the experience. Instead of wasting 10 years trying to accomplish your goals, why not take a shortcut and have a coach guide you along the way?

5. Coaches help you navigate the five key areas of business you need to succeed in. I learned this from a business coach I hired, Alex Charfen:

- Lead generation - How are you getting leads each week?
- Lead nurture - How are you nurturing the leads to become buyers?
- Conversion - How are you going to close the sale?
- Delivery - How good are you at delivering the product or service to the customer?
- Retention/Upsell - How good are you at retaining current clients and increasing their 'cart value'? The easiest way to increase your revenue is to get current customers to buy more from you.

6. A business coach can be someone to vent to about things in the business that you can't talk to your leadership team about. Maybe it's a financial crisis or something personal happening in your life that's affecting your work. As leaders and business owners, you can't be the one that falls apart. You have to be strong for the group, so you need someone you can process different situations with and lean on in times of struggle. This also alleviates you going home and venting everything to your spouse, which could negatively affect that relationship and your work-life balance. A coach lets you vent, process the information and come up with a plan to improve the situation.

7. A coach will open your mind to new habits and ideas. Coaches who have worked with hundreds of clients over the years can give you insight on strategies that worked with their other clients in different industries. This is one of the most valuable tools that a coach can give you.
Finding a coach who has achieved what you want to achieve in your career will help you fast track your way to success. When choosing a coach, I would steer clear of coaches who have not actually accomplished what you want to do with your business. Make sure you're very aware of their background, accomplishments and credentials before deciding to be mentored by them. You want someone who can empathize with you and properly guide you on your journey.
I've worked with coaches over the years who have opened my eyes to where I could improve on the operations side of my business. Often, this involved me taking a step back and delegating more tasks to my team. As entrepreneurs, we often think we're the only ones who can get the job done, but this just isn't true. It's hard when you're the one with the vision who built the business, but you have to step back and play the role of the visionary – the one who strategically plans for growth – rather than handling the day-to-day of the business. This approach will pay dividends for the growth of your business, and it's one I didn't implement until I consulted with a business coach I trusted.

If you're thinking about hiring a business coach but aren't sure if now is the time, I offer free, 15-minute consultations. Just click the 'Get a quote' button at www.D2Branding.com.

I want to share the stories of four amazing women I have coached on creating personal branding businesses:

Truth DEI, Nona Lee

I met Nona Lee doing a LinkedIn outreach marketing campaign. Nona was my ideal avatar, a female executive who was tired of working long hours and was ready for time freedom, while doing something that provided her purpose in life.

Nona spent 22 years as an Executive Vice President and Legal Officer for the Arizona Diamondbacks. She was burnt out at her job, worked a ton of hours and felt like she had a bigger purpose in her life, but wasn't sure what that was at the time. After several coaching sessions, I discovered that Nona was really passionate about diversity, equity and inclusion in the workplace. She was the only gay, black, female executive that worked in Major League Baseball at the time and had experienced her fair share of discrimination and exclusion throughout her life. She knew DEI was extremely important to her, but wasn't sure how to make it a business. After six months of coaching, I helped her launch Truth DEI Consulting, a firm focused on educating organizations on diversity, equity and inclusion to improve business culture and increase the bottom line. In less than one year, Truth DEI has added nine speakers and consultants to their team and also launched Truth Retreats, an immersive civil journey to truth and reconciliation in Montgomery, Alabama. Nona has been honored to work with clients such as the Gates Foundation, Disney, Hewlett Packard, and more.

One of the greatest things you can do in marketing is have other people share their results from working with you. Here's what Nona had to say:

> "Deedra Determan and her team at D2 Branding are the best in the business. Deedra is a highly experienced, knowledgeable, and passionate professional, and so much more! She is a thoughtful and creative visionary when it comes to building brands and businesses. She and her team got to know me, listened intently to my vision, researched my industry, and helped me strategically shape, build and launch Truth DEI in a way that has been as successful as she said it would be. I absolutely could not have done it without her and her team. It was well worth the investment. If you are starting a new business or rebranding your current business, I

highly recommend that you work with Deedra and D2 Branding. You will not be disappointed!"

Nona Lee
Founder/CEO - Truth DEI Consulting

Delphi Strategies, Adrienne Ramsay

I also met Adrienne Ramsay on LinkedIn through a marketing outreach campaign we were doing at D2 Branding. My target was female CEOs and entrepreneurs. Adrienne was currently a business consultant with a couple of clients, but hadn't been able to scale her business. She did not have a brand, logo, or a website created, she was just going off word-of-mouth. Adrienne spent years as a senior executive with high-technology start-ups in the government service, aerospace and national security industries with a proven track record in public policy. She had an impressive background but needed a brand to give her credibility. Adrienne participated in my six-month personal branding coaching program, and we launched Delphi Strategies, a corporate management and innovation consulting and advisory firm for high-technology organizations and start-ups. By Adrienne creating a personal brand, she was able to bring credibility to her impressive experience to land big clients.

"I have been working with Deedra Determan and D2 Branding for the past year building my personal brand, creating my online consulting business, and launching my website and social media presence! Every week I know I am closer to my personal goals and Deedra and her team are key players in this journey! The meetings are always structured and focused on goals and results. Deedra's coaching has enabled me to create a problem-solving framework with all the teaching materials and launch

my management consulting practice with clarity of purpose and vision.
Working with Deedra is one of the best things I have done with my time, energy, and resources!
500 stars!!!"

Adrienne Ramsay
Founder - Delphi Strategies

Dyfference Makers, Laken Gooch

Laken Gooch was a teacher who had a 3rd grade son with dyslexia. He was struggling in school and no one seemed to know how to teach him in a way he could understand. After years of frustration, Laken came to me with a vision to start a nonprofit to help kids with dyslexia learn how to read and write with confidence. After finishing my personal branding coaching program, Laken launched a non-profit, Discover the Dyfference, Inc. Her organization provides online curriculum and instruction to struggling readers and those with dyslexia, based on the research-based program, the Science of Reading. The Dyfference Makers Academy, is both affordable and flexible in schedule, offering real authentic help to kids, parents and families. This online learning platform allows Laken to work from home and incorporate her work with her own son into the teaching videos. We created the name, logo, website, video, coaching program and pricing structure. Laken was a great candidate to develop a personal brand around her being a teacher and mom with a son who struggled in school due to dyslexia. Laken recorded hundreds of videos for her online curriculum using her kids and even their dog, Dunder, to help kids across the country learn. Dyfference Makers strives to raise awareness and advocate for those affected by dyslexia, while simultaneously empowering struggling readers and their families.

Laken had this to say about the coaching program:

> "Deedra and her all-star team have been instrumental in helping us create our non-profit from the ground up. They constantly helped guide and encourage us throughout the entire process from developing our brand story to creating our website and social media presence. We would not have been able to achieve our goal of advocating and helping struggling readers without Deedra's coaching expertise. We highly recommend D2 Branding for any business and/or nonprofit needs."
>
> **Kent & Laken Gooch**
> Dyfference Makers

Steffanie Bonner Consulting, Steffanie Bonner

Steffanie Bonner had more than 25 years of experience working at nonprofits. When I met her she was working for a credit union where she had launched a charitable foundation for them. Steffanie's goal was to work the hours she wanted to work while making the money she wanted to make using her experience to help nonprofits. She was tired of working hard for other people and not having flexibility in her schedule. After completing my personal branding coaching program, we launched Steffanie Bonner Consulting, a nonprofit consulting firm empowering nonprofits to increase their mission through capital campaigns, fundraising, and organizational development. I helped Steffanie create her brand, define her avatar (ideal client), create and price her coaching program, and establish a strategic marketing and sales plan to get clients. She recently was able to quit her job to pursue her personal branding business full time.

Here's what Steffanie had to say:

> "Deedra and her team are top-notch! I highly recommend her personal branding program to help launch your dream career. Her team of professionals work together to create your brand through website development, creative design, social media presence and marketing."
>
> **Steffanie Bonner**
> Founder, Steffanie Bonner Consulting

Section 2: Now It's Time to Talk About You

By now, you know all of the things to do at the start of your business: how to invest in yourself and the company, how to grow your business, build a team of rockstars, avoid financial mistakes, make money, and find a business coach to grow and scale! You are well on your way to building a successful personal branding business! There's just one thing left: developing YOU!

The good news is there is only one thing that can get in the way of growing and scaling your business: YOU! After years of coaching CEOs and entrepreneurs, I came up with a list of 20 things that will get in the way of your success if you don't fix them now! We can all follow a game plan but these are common issues I see that get in the way of my clients' dreams.

THINGS THAT GET IN THE WAY OF YOUR SUCCESS

1. LACK OF CONFIDENCE: YOU HAVE TO BE THE QUEEN OF CONFIDENCE
2. INCONSISTENCY: IF YOU AREN'T CONSISTENT, YOU'LL NEVER WIN
3. NEGATIVE BELIEFS: HOW TO CREATE A MILLIONAIRE MINDSET
4. IMPOSTER SYNDROME: IF YOU DON'T BELIEVE IN YOURSELF, WHO WILL?
5. LACK OF ENERGY: DO YOU NEED AN ENERGY SHIFT
6. AVOIDING DIFFICULT CONVERSATIONS
7. OVERTHINKING EVERYTHING
8. PROCRASTINATION: WHY DO WE PROCRASTINATE EVEN WHEN WE KNOW IT WILL HURT US
9. BEING LAZY: 10 WAYS TO BEAT LAZINESS & BE PRODUCTIVE
10. FEAR: THE THREE BIGGEST FEARS WOMEN CEOS & ENTREPRENEURS FACE
11. BURNOUT: FEELING BURNED OUT? FIVE WAYS TO RECHARGE
12. LACK OF A SCHEDULE: YOU HAVE TO SCHEDULE EVERYTHING!
13. LACK OF EMOTIONAL INTELLIGENCE: HOW YOUR EI AFFECTS YOUR BUSINESS
14. ALWAYS PLAYING DEFENSE: ARE YOU PLAYING OFFENSE OR DEFENSE IN YOUR BUSINESS
15. FEAR OF DOING HARD THINGS: WANT TO SUCCEED? DO HARD THINGS.
16. TAKING EVERYTHING PERSONALLY: WHY DO WE ALWAYS TAKE IT PERSONAL
17. FEAR OF TAKING ACTION: QUIT TALKING ABOUT IT. DO IT.

Things That Get in the Way of Your Success, #1

Lack of Confidence: You Have to Be the Queen of Confidence

The risk you regret most in life is the one you didn't take!

Why are some people so confident and others struggle to believe in themselves? It always amazes me when I meet an entrepreneur who is crazy confident and hasn't really done anything in business to give them that confidence and then others who have been wildly successful yet they still lack confidence and don't think they are good enough for success. I see a lack of confidence more in the women I coach versus the men.

Confidence is the most beautiful thing you can possess! You have to show up every single day like you were meant to be at that particular moment like it is your purpose in life!

I read a book years ago called Lean In by Sheryl Sandberg and she says that men walk into a job interview with 25% knowledge and 100% confidence and women come to the same interview with 100% knowledge and 25% confidence. Why is this? I want to change this! There is absolutely no reason for this!

Most of the time when you compliment another woman, they downplay it and respond with something negative about themselves. Try it and you will see what I mean. You say, wow you look great! They usually say something like, "Yeah, well I need to lose about 20 pounds," instead of just confidently responding, "Thank you!"

This is a great lesson to teach your daughter and practice it yourself! The next time someone compliments you, smile and say THANK YOU!

Think about when you were a kid. Some kids are naturally very confident at anything they try to do while others who may even have the skills, lack confidence. Was it the way we were raised? I do think parents, teachers and peers have a lot to do with that early on and some people go their whole lives with a limited belief in themselves and their abilities.

I was blessed to have two parents who made me believe I could do anything I wanted to do. I never went into a tryout in sports or for a job interview thinking I couldn't succeed. I knew I could do it! I knew I had the talent and most importantly, I believed in myself. Transferring this type of confidence to anyone you interact with in business is so important! Whether it's a sales call, an interview, or a conversation with a current client, confidence is such a powerful trait that everyone admires. Confidence is not at all the same thing as pride, which communicates a "better than" attitude. Instead, confidence is believing in who you are as a person and what you bring to the table.

One of the most powerful things I can do for my clients is to give them confidence to reach their dreams! I love to build people up, highlight their strengths, and cheer them on to success! Many times that's the only thing missing from them reaching their goals! You can't take risks if you aren't confident! What are you missing out on because you are scared? I spend most of my time reassuring clients that they are the expert and they have the knowledge that other people want.

Here are 5 tips to being confident in business and in life!

1. Be decisive!

One of the traits that will kill your entrepreneurial journey is being indecisive. You have to just ACT! Decision-making should be something that's taught in college. I see it paralyze so many people. They just can't decide whether to create this product or that product or what audience they want to go after. I remind them: It's not a forever decision! You aren't married to it, just ACT and if it doesn't work, PIVOT! I am more of an impulsive person who acts quickly without a ton of thought. That may not always be the right thing, as there are plenty of things I probably should have thought out more, but it has served me more good in my life than bad. Practice being decisive! I have friends who can't decide where to go eat or what they are going to wear and will literally spend HOURS contemplating these simple things in life! Decide and move on! A confident person is a decisive person.

2. Don't let fear dictate your actions!

What is fear anyway? It is a human emotion that starts in your imagination! Most of the time there is nothing to be fearful of - it is something you imagined and gave meaning to! If you let fear creep into your life, it will 100% control you! The best thing you can do with fear is FACE IT! I was coaching a female entrepreneur the other day who was so fearful of making sales calls. She is the expert, has an amazing program, but lost all of her confidence and was filled with fear to get on a call. Clients definitely sense your fear and lack of confidence so you cannot be in this state of mind when you are on a sales call. We ended up role playing the sales call over and over until she was confident and she got the sale! Closing sales will give you confidence, but I told her she won't close all of them. It takes repetition to get confidence, and sales is a numbers game! The more you pitch, the more you close, the more confident you become!

3. Quit being a perfectionist!
You don't have to have everything perfect before you launch. I always tell people if I waited to have my kids until my life was perfect, I wouldn't be a mom. Sure, we all want a successful job and the ideal house before we bring children into the world, but that rarely happens! And a child doesn't care about any of that! They want your love!

The same thing goes for business. So many people wait to launch until they have the perfect website and marketing materials and keep taking course after course to improve their skills. Guess what? Your opportunity is going to be gone! Your competitor will scoop up the available market share while you are waiting for perfection. Have the confidence to LAUNCH! Imperfect action is better than no action at all! You can tweak along the way, and nine times out of 10, the honest feedback you will get is from customers, and you can make adjustments as you go! You won't get this kind of feedback until you launch!

4. Stop worrying about what other people think!
The older I get, the less I care what others think of me. I am not here on Earth to please everyone. It used to be hard for me in business when I pitched a potential client, and they would go with another agency. WHY? Did they not like me? Did I not clearly explain how we can change their life? The more I did sales, the more I realized it wasn't always about me. Or maybe it was about me, but it didn't matter! I didn't need to be the marketing expert for everyone in the world. Once I created a niche and stuck with that niche, I had success. And it was a relief only working with those clients I wanted to work with.

Many people spend so much time worrying about what their competitors are doing and then try to copy them. Be original! Those who are successful have no idea what their competitors are posting on social media or even care! There's enough business for everyone to be successful, not just one. Comparing your company to others will get you nowhere. They have their journey, and you have yours. Live out your journey to the fullest. Have the confidence in your business to stay the course, regardless of what your competition is doing.

The worst thing you can do in a sales pitch is worry about what the other person is thinking. Be confident! Who cares if they go another route? I've often pitched a client, didn't land the deal, and they later called me to do business. Maybe I was too expensive, or the timing wasn't right, but it does me no good to worry about what other people think. I DO IT MY WAY, and keep moving forward!

5. Take care of yourself!

When was the last time you did something for yourself? I know many female entrepreneurs put themselves last. They run their businesses, their clients, their team members, their spouses, and their kids...after taking care of all of that, there's not much left for themselves!

You have to create time to recharge and feel better about yourself! Maybe this is working out; maybe it's meditating or going for a walk. Do something every day for you! You cannot be 100% with your clients or family unless you feel 100%!

I am very guarded with my time for this reason. I have my workout time at 5 am every morning. That is "me" time to feel strong and confident and get those endorphins flowing! Then, I have "me" time in the morning when I get to work an hour before anyone else. This is when I read, listen to podcasts, or shop online. I do something I want to do for personal development, whatever that looks like. I also consistently go to bed by

9pm. I know this is not for everyone, but my body needs consistent sleep, and getting up at 4:30 am is not easy. I cannot be at my best if I don't get the sleep I need, so every night at about 8 pm, I leave my phone in my bathroom so I have no distractions for the night. My friends laugh at me that I can't stay up past 10 pm even on the weekends (yes, I do sleep in until at least 6:30 or seven on weekends), but I rarely get sick and have stuck to this routine for years.

I am also a big fan of rewarding myself when I reach my business goals. As entrepreneurs, we don't have bosses to congratulate or give us raises, so we have to reward ourselves! Come up with a goal and what you will do when you achieve it. Maybe it's a tropical vacation with your spouse or that new Louis Vuitton you've been eyeing. Set your goal, and GO GET IT! Guilt Free! You deserve it!

You are much more confident when you are well-rested and take care of yourself!

To recap, here are the five things you need to be a confident person!

1. Be Decisive
2. Don't let fear dictate your actions
3. Quit being a perfectionist
4. Stop worrying about what other people think
5. Take care of yourself

Now, go be the queen of confidence! You are valuable, and other people need you. Make the calls, put in the work, and reward yourself along the way!

Things That Get in the Way of Your Success, #2

Inconsistency: If You Aren't Consistent, You'll Never Win!

Consistency wins, period.

You can pay for expensive business coaches, sign up for every personal development program you can find, read every entrepreneurship book out there, and have an incredible business plan. Still, if you don't execute your plan consistently, you'll never win.

Consistency means making daily sales calls to get new business, creating a social media content plan and posting regularly, and nurturing current clients how they deserve to be nurtured. Consistency is making these things part of your everyday workflow and not doing them just when you feel like it.

Consistency is the secret sauce when it comes to being successful. When people ask how I got to where I am today, I always tell them I have never been the most intelligent person in the room, but I am consistent.

That means that ten years after launching D2 Branding, I'm still on weekly sales calls to get new clients. I could easily be complacent and say, "I'm making good money, and the business is doing well, so I'm going to take it easy this week and relax." That approach won't yield good results in the long run, though. You have to constantly be adding to your bottom line and coming up with new ways to generate revenue.

That means that even after 10 years, I still write out my weekly commitments every Sunday. I don't have a boss asking me for it, and no one would know if I didn't do it, but I wouldn't be able to accomplish all of the things I need to have a successful business if I didn't have a consistent weekly plan.

This also means that for the past 25 years, I've gotten up and worked out six days a week at 5 a.m. I work out consistently, every day, even when I don't feel like it because my health is too important to me not to. Staying healthy and in good shape ensures I can live a fulfilled life. What fun is it if you have a million dollars but aren't well enough to travel and do things you want with friends and family? Taking care of myself by consistently working out and making healthy meals is how I ensure I'm the best version of myself, personally and professionally.

To bring even more consistency into my professional life, I continuously try to educate myself about my industry because marketing constantly changes. We can all learn more, and I don't know everything I need to know. If I were still approaching marketing the same way I was, even just three to five years ago, D2 would not be successful or even be in business. I am constantly learning about new marketing trends and trying new social media strategies for our clients. This is how I stay on top of things and ensure we are ahead of the curve.

Being consistent with my family is one of my most important things. This is why every Sunday, we have a family dinner. It might not always be fancy, but it's consistent, and it provides a space for us to reconnect with each other as we go into the new week.

What are the things that are most important to you? To reach your goals, you have to map out a plan to get there. There's no magic formula, and you don't need to be a rocket scientist to figure it out. Just make a plan and stick to it consistently! You also don't have to be super bright to work hard and be consistent. Anyone can do it!

A client told me the other day that they had no idea what to do, that they were stuck and needed my help. I thought to myself, 'You actually don't need my help!' They knew their goals, they knew their plan, and they knew what they had to do each day to reach their goals. It's not fun, it's not exciting, and it's not always easy, but you know what you need to do – you just have to make yourself do it! Consistency can seem tedious, but it's how you get results.

Consistency starts with you! You are the driver behind your business, and how your time is spent is totally up to you!

Here are some critical steps you need to take to create consistency in your business:

Set your goals. If you don't know where you want to go, how will you get there? How many hours do you want to work per day? How much money do you need to make to live the life you want to live? Ask yourself the critical questions so you can get a better idea of what you want to accomplish. Come up with a plan. If clients are what you're after, determine how many you'll need to reach your monthly revenue goal, break down how many sales calls it will take to get that many clients, and how many calls you need each day to reach that goal. If you're trying to gain followers, develop a content plan to get you there.

Execute the plan. Plan your day to ensure you get the most important things done first, then make time for the less crucial things afterward. When you plan out your professional commitments as well as your personal time, you're able to manage your time much better.

There will inevitably be days when you need to pivot, but if you can, stick to your consistent plan as much as possible! By adhering to your plan each day, you're getting closer and closer to the goals you want to reach.

Remember: Consistency wins!

Things That Get in the Way of Your Success, #3

Negative Beliefs: How to Create a MILLIONAIRE Mindset

Being in control of your thoughts will influence how you live your life.

The clients I work with who can control their mindset are always the ones who are more successful.

Things will always happen that are out of your control, and every day will have its own set of challenges. You're not going to have a great day every single day. You can, however, control how you respond to whatever each day throws at you.

One of my favorite quotes is from Napoleon Hill, author of the book Think and Grow Rich: "If you fail to control your own mind, you may be sure that you will control nothing else."

When you train your mind for success, you'll have the ability to overcome any obstacles that come your way.

I've watched this scenario play out a hundred times: A talented, innovative entrepreneur with all the tools they need to succeed except a positive mindset and a less gifted person who lacks some of the resources they need to succeed, yet they have a positive mindset. Who do you think comes out on top? The person with a positive mindset because they believe in themselves and will do whatever it takes to succeed.

We've all been around people who are Debbie Downers, looking at life through a negative lens. These people can suck the life out of you if you let them. Have you ever found yourself complaining along with them without even realizing it? That happens when you surround yourself with the wrong people in the wrong environment.

I recently met with a coaching client with everything she needs to succeed. She's already built a solid personal brand and has a fantastic following of members in a private Facebook group who all love her content. The group is active, and they want what she has to offer, but she still lets self-doubt creep in, causing her to stop engaging in the group. She lets the negative thoughts in her mind take over and allows them to impede her progress and derail her momentum.

Things like this will happen in your career occasionally, and it's normal, but you can't let it throw you off the path you've worked so hard to pave for yourself. When mental blocks arise, things go wrong, or negative thoughts start to creep in, you have to get back up, put a smile on your face, and retrain your mind to visualize the potential positive outcomes. You have to picture yourself at the top of your game, making the money you want to make and living your best life.

It might feel unnatural initially, but you have to start shifting your mindset to reflect the belief that you were made to succeed. After all, someone will succeed in your niche market, so why shouldn't it be you? I don't wake up every morning feeling like a rockstar who will conquer the day, but I do know how to get myself into that state of mind: by creating an authentic-to-me morning routine that sets me up for success.

My morning routine involves waking up early, working out, getting ready, and listening to an uplifting podcast or music. I get to the office early so I'm not stressed about my day, and I make a plan for what I'm going to do first. I find that the busier I am, the more productive I am.

It's essential to create an environment both at work and in your personal life that supports your growth. Negativity breeds negativity, so pay close attention to your environment and the people you spend time with. Are they uplifting and supportive of your endeavors, or do they tear you down and complain about life? We all have people that we're forced to be around who may be negative (a family member, neighbor, or mom at your kid's school), and there's no getting away from them. What do you do when the negative talk starts? Don't feed into it. Instead, change the subject or say something positive about the situation. If you always turn a negative into a positive, they will start to realize it and won't complain around you anymore.

Why do some people seem to have it all? The successful business, the perfect family, the ideal body - it seems they have everything they want while others can't catch a break. It all comes down to their mindset: If you think you can accomplish greatness, you will achieve greatness. On the other hand, if you think you will lose, you probably will.

My daughter's high school soccer team played in the state finals a few years ago. I talked with my daughter and some of her teammates before the game. Both teams were incredibly talented - on any given day, one could win the game over the other. It would ultimately come down to who wanted it more and who had the winning mindset. We've all heard stories of professional athletes visualizing themselves winning before they ever step foot on the court or field. I gave my daughter that advice: Visualize yourself playing the absolute best game of your life, running as fast as you can, stopping every ball that comes your way - and that's exactly what she did! They won three-to-two, securing the state title. The skill level shown by both teams on the field was equal, but her team wanted it more. They fought hard and had a winning mindset before the game even started.

What a great lesson in life: Visualize it before it happens! Visualize yourself living in your dream home with financial freedom, getting to do the things you love to do. This is the most essential step in becoming a successful entrepreneur.

Here are five proven ways to keep a positive mindset:

1. Embrace your existence in the present moment instead of always thinking there is something better or that you will be happy when you reach a particular milestone. As an entrepreneur, you are never finished. Celebrate all of your successes along the way.

2. You can be your own worst critic or your own biggest fan. You are in control of your thoughts! Don't let other people's comments shape the way you view yourself. Try to avoid harping on:
    - What your parents or other kids in school told you growing up.
    - Comparing yourself to others who are successful in your field.
    - Things you tell yourself based on past rejection.

3. You become what you think. If you are constantly thinking negatively, you will become that. Start every day with positive affirmations about yourself, your career, your family, and your life! We all have so much to be grateful for, so instead of thinking of all of the things we don't have, think of all of the positive things we do have! Enjoy the journey!

4. You can create a positive state by controlling your thoughts. If you have a negative thought enter your

head, cast it down with a positive thought until you train your mind.

5. Turn failures into opportunities to learn and improve for next time!

Visualize success - It activates the law of attraction, thereby drawing into your life the people, support, and circumstances you will need to realize your goals! How do you create a positive mindset every day?

Things That Get in the Way of Your Success, #4

Imposter Syndrome: If You Don't Believe in Yourself, Who Will?

Have you ever felt like you weren't qualified to do something?

I hear this sentiment all the time from my clients. They get close to launching their business or their personal brand, and they start to let self-doubt creep in. Suddenly, they don't feel qualified to launch their business, or they come up with an excuse as to why they're not ready to start. Often, they compare themselves to their competition and let insecurity affect their drive. It's easy to compare yourself to everyone who's ahead of you in the game, to all the people who have successful businesses doing something similar to what you're doing.

I try not to think about my competition because I've found that it isn't helpful. There are so many marketing companies out there, and I could have easily never launched my business because someone had already done what I was about to do. The truth is, though, while there are many digital marketing experts, not everyone has my skills, knowledge, background, and story. That's why it's essential to create a personal brand. That is what makes D2 Branding unique!

Imposter syndrome is a real thing, and I started to see more and more of it when I started working with personal brands. Your personal brand, after all, is you. You have to be confident in your skills and direction, but it's hard to have confidence when you haven't gotten one client yet. Even if you're well-qualified, there's a different kind of pressure when your name is attached to the business. You're no longer on a corporate team contributing – 100% of the company's outcome is up to you. This challenge can be scary and can create self-doubt if you let it.

The first thing I tell people is to remember why they're launching their business in the first place. I want them to focus on who they're helping and what difference they're making in the world. After all, it's not about you; it's about who you're helping. If you keep that at the front of your mind, you won't care what people think about your actions.

The great thing about launching a personal brand is that you don't have to be perfect for everyone. It's actually better if you're not. I encourage people to create a niche and to only go after people like them (their dream clients). You don't need everyone to love you or buy from you. But what if you could tap into just 1% of your industry? You'd probably be massively successful.

If you feel like you aren't qualified to do your job or launch your business, that is normal. We all have feelings of self-doubt in our lives, but you can't live in that state of mind.

Here are some steps to help you overcome those feelings:

1. **Reframe your mindset.** Don't worry about what people might think of you, especially those who aren't even your target audience. Think of the people who need what you have and who you will be helping with your product or service.

2. List your skills and what makes you qualified to do what you do. What 5-10 things have you accomplished that have gotten you to where you are today? We all have these benchmarks, so dig deep and make a list. You might even ask past colleagues or your partner about your most significant strengths to get an outside perspective. Put this list on your phone or on your bathroom mirror, and read it every day. You are more than qualified to do what you do, and there are people on the other side who need you!

3. Don't compare yourself to anyone else. No one has your exact skills and knowledge, and no one is on the same path as you. If you put your head down, do the work, and trust your instincts, you'll be successful. Don't waste too much time comparing your journey to anyone else's.

4. Highlight the things that make you different. Your brand and your story are unique; own that. If you are true to yourself, you will attract the right client.

5. Let go of being perfect. No one is perfect, and there's no ideal time to launch your business. Now is the time! If we all waited to take action until everything in our lives was perfect, we would never do anything. Celebrate your successes along the way, and when a mistake happens, figure out what you could do differently next time and move on. Perfectionism is exhausting, and no one is perfect. Remember, it's better to launch with imperfections than to never launch at all!

If you are starting to feel imposter syndrome kick in, stop what you are doing and go back and read your list. You are unique, you have a story to tell, and people need what you have to offer.

The key is to move forward, cast down negative thoughts, and keep moving. Launch that business and create that personal brand – the world can benefit from what you're offering.

Things That Get in the Way of Your Success, #5

Lack of Energy: Do You Need an Energy Shift?

Have you ever met someone who had tremendous energy? You want to be around that person and feed off their energy all the time. They make everyone around them feel great and bring vitality to any situation.

Having contagious energy like this can be influential in business. As a business coach, I set the energy in a coaching session whenever I meet with my client. Some days, I may not feel like it, but it's my job. And I find that when I start to bring the energy, I begin to feel better, too.

Think about energy on a sales call or in a pitch meeting. Your energy in that interaction sets the tone immediately and allows you to direct the conversation, increasing your chances of selling. Your energy should bring you into a flow state, where it feels more like you're conversing with a friend than a potential client. Whoever is on the other end of your pitch should forget that you're selling to them and feel more like you're having a conversation together. If you can use your energy to connect with anyone, you will be successful.

If you can learn to create your own energy and channel it, great things will happen. Big decisions generate a change in energy. Just like finally leaving a job you've been wanting to quit for years, there's a sense of relief and a surge of power when you make the move that your soul has been dying for. Every day, week, and year that passes by without you making a decision you know you need to make causes you to lose vital energy. The moment the decision is made, however, your energy shifts because you've moved into alignment with what's best for you.

Everyone has a source of energy that fuels them. It's the strength you draw from to overcome obstacles. But most of us aren't aware of what makes us powerful or how we can show our abilities most effectively. The problem is that we don't tend to see ourselves as capable, dynamic, forceful, or influential. We dwell on our faults and mistakes, and this takes our energy from us, making our positive energy slip away. Remember, you control your energy. If there are things in your life that are taking energy away from you, you need to eliminate them. Maybe you're stuck in a job you hate or are dealing with a negative coworker. Coping with this negative energy day in and day out will drain you.

Over the next week, carry a notebook with you or use your phone to document the negative energy you encounter. At the same time, look for the positive people and things that fill you up. As you look at the negative list, ask yourself what you can eliminate today, in a month, or a year. What do you have the power to change? Make a goal to eliminate these things from your life. From the list of people and things that bring you positive energy, where can you get more of that? Maybe you have a mentor or a friend who always makes you feel better. Can you get coffee with them once a week? This will give you perspective on the people and things you need to surround yourself with moving forward.

Here are some tips to increase the positive energy in your life:

1. **Exercise in the morning** to increase your energy throughout the day. Studies have shown that those who workout first thing in the morning have increased energy levels that sustain them.

2. **Declutter your space.** It's hard to bring energy to work daily if your workspace is cluttered. It automatically puts your mind in a stressful state. Decluttering your area before you leave for the day will set you up for success the next day. The same principle applies to your home. If you come home to a messy house with an unmade bed, your stress levels will rise. Wake up a few minutes early so you have time to make your bed and clean up any mess you've made so you come home to a peaceful house.

3. **Take care of your nutrition.** Healthy food choices like lean proteins, whole grains, and plenty of veggies boost energy from the inside out. Same with drinking plenty of water. Processed, high-sugar, high-fat foods quite literally weigh you down and make you feel sluggish throughout the day.

4. **Listen to music** or put on an inspiring podcast to help you increase your energy levels before you walk into work or jump on a sales call. Even if you have to sit in the parking lot at work and listen to something that gets you pumped up, do it – it'll start your day off right.

5. **Focus on the outcome!** Think about the effects of bringing your best energy to the office daily. Your clients and co-workers will be excited to see you, your children will respond differently when you ask them to do something, and your boss/coworkers will positively think of you. Everyone around you is affected by your energy.

How will you show up today?

Things That Get in the Way of Your Success, #6

Avoiding Difficult Conversations!

As a boss, you'll inevitably have to have hard conversations. When you're in charge, your time is money. How you allocate your time will affect your bottom line, so you don't have time to stew over difficult conversations. It would help if you had a plan in place for when situations like these come up so you can deal with them effectively and efficiently.

We've all been in a situation where there's a member of your team who is underperforming and, in turn, negatively affecting the entire team. Maybe you have a client who is upset and is mistreating your employees because of it. Perhaps one of your competitors is overstepping boundaries by copying your business model, marketing approach, or website copy. You could even have two employees who aren't getting along and are creating a culture of gossiping within the workplace.

None of these situations are ideal, but they will most likely happen under you at some point if you're in a leadership position. If you're scaling your company and adding more employees and clients, there will almost always be some conflict that comes up.

I've had all of these scenarios happen at different points throughout my career, and it's taught me that the more I avoid having difficult conversations, the more problematic and complex they are to solve. These problems are like wildfires: if they aren't contained immediately, they'll continue to grow, and you'll get burned.

Here are five ways to have difficult conversations at work so you can have the best possible outcomes.

1. **Practice empathy.**
   I had to fire a beloved employee once, which broke my heart. D2 is a small company, so we know everything about each other — what everyone's kids are doing, where they go on vacation, and more. That's one of the best things about having a small business, but it can also make things very difficult when you have to make a change in the team. In this particular situation, this team member wasn't a right fit for our company. We tried transitioning her into several different positions, but nothing was working out. I took responsibility for hiring the wrong person for the job, but in my conversation with her, I had to step back and look at the situation from her point of view. She had a family, bills to pay, and other responsibilities, so I gave her ample time to transition and even found her a job with one of my clients that she was better suited for. When it comes time to have a difficult conversation at work, try to put yourself in the other person's shoes and empathize with what they might be going through.

2. **Be honest.**
   In business, I've learned that the more you sugarcoat a situation, the more unclear your message will be, leading to confusion and hurt feelings. In the past, I've tried to have vague conversations with team members when they were not meeting our standards. I wasn't being

direct, so the team members went back to doing exactly what they were doing before. Instead of beating around the bush, spell it out clearly (and slowly) and offer a solution. Maybe they need additional training or mentorship to succeed in their role. Honesty is always the best workplace policy, and your team members will respect you for it. Tell them directly what you need from them so they know how to step up.

3. Choose people over money.
I once had a client who treated our team poorly. They talked down to team members and were disrespectful, but I tolerated it for months because they were our largest-paying client. I almost had a team member quit over it and realized that the money wasn't worth the suffering. I had to have a difficult (and months overdue) conversation with the client. To my surprise, the client didn't realize they were coming across the way they were, and their attitude improved drastically. Prioritize your team members and stick up for them. It's better to focus on maintaining a solid and loyal team around you than to be overly focused on money.

4. Communicate your policies upfront.
I once had a client who was two months late on their billing and owed me over $5,000, which was coming directly out of my pocket. This client was someone who I considered a friend. I knew they were waiting on a big payment in their business to be able to pay me, but I let it go on much longer than I should have. I had to have a difficult conversation with them where I let them know that we were cutting off all of their marketing and not working on their website until we were paid. These conversations are not fun, but they are necessary. I now have a policy in place that if a client's credit card doesn't go through, we contact them. If we don't get a response within 24 hours, we stop our work until it can

be reconciled. If you have a policy that's communicated up front, there will be no surprise if you have to take that action down the road.

5. **Reflect on how you did.**
After a difficult conversation, it's worthwhile to reflect and consider what went well and what didn't. Consider why you had specific reactions and what you should have said differently. It's also always good to follow up with an email documenting the conversation to avoid confusion.

Avoiding difficult conversations is never a good way to solve problems. Have hard discussions early, then move on to get your head back into the game.

Things That Get in the Way of Your Success, #7

Overthinking Everything

People often cannot be their best at work or personal lives because they overthink everything. In my experience, overthinking in your professional life doesn't benefit you in any way – it does the opposite; it holds you back.

An example of this experience may be overthinking proposals you pitch to potential clients. Instead of spending two weeks crafting a proposal, you're better off putting something together quickly and pitching it. If you wait too long, you risk your client not being that interested anymore. When a client says they're interested in my offer, I send a proposal that day. This tactic works well because what I'm offering them is still fresh in their minds. Nine times out of ten, you'll get the sale by moving quicker.

Another thing many people in business find themselves overthinking is what they post on social media. I have a client who is a highly credentialed expert in her field. Despite her qualifications, anytime she creates a post or creates a video to advise her followers, she second-guesses herself. I understand where she's coming from because I'm guilty of doing this. If you want to grow your business and social media presence, however, you have to let go of that fear. If you're going after a niche audience, they want to hear what you have to say, and pictures and videos of yourself will always perform better than words or graphics because they feel much more personal and grab people's attention. Don't get upset if you don't get many likes or engagement on your content at first. Keep posting, stay consistent, and remember that people need what you have.

It's also common for people to overthink their websites. I have a client who hasn't launched their website for a year because it isn't perfect. Guess what's better than perfect? A live website! For a year, this client has missed out on leads because she's holding her website to too high of a standard and overthinking every aspect. This inaction has cost her business.

The biggest thing my clients tend to overthink is sales – and I don't blame them. It's easy to overthink sales. You might call, text, or email someone several times and get no response. This rejection can feel devastating, and it's easy to take it personally. What you need to remember is that rejection probably doesn't have anything to do with you. The timing might not be correct, or they might be too busy to respond. For every 100 people you reach out to, you might only get 10 responses – and that's ok! Work with what you get back, keep your head up, and keep going.

I came up with a list of six ways to stop overthinking and start doing.

1. **Be aware of when you're overthinking.** Awareness is the first step in stopping a behavior.

2. **Don't think of everything that can go wrong**. Instead, picture everything going right. Don't live with your glass half-empty. It's not a positive state to live in.

3. **Keep yourself busy with things** that make you feel

happy and engaged. Maybe it's exercise, reading a book, or helping someone in need. It's hard to focus on yourself and overthink when helping someone else.

4. Stop telling yourself stories that aren't true. Ask yourself if what you're worried about will matter to you in a year or five years. If it won't matter, move on!

5. Don't wait for everything to be "perfect" to get started. This is one of the most debilitating problems for business owners. Remember, imperfect action is better than no action at all.

6. Start a gratitude journal and write down what you're thankful for every day. If your heart is filled with gratitude and appreciation, you won't have time to overthink and worry.

Bottom line: Stop overthinking and start making decisions. Entrepreneurs who make quick decisions are more likely to have success than those who sit around and overthink everything.

Things That Get in the Way of Your Success, #8

Procrastination: Why Do We Procrastinate, Even When We Know it Will Hurt Us?

We can probably all think of times when we've put off doing something we know we need to do. Maybe it's having a difficult conversation with an employee, or perhaps it's starting a fitness journey or nutrition plan. Or, maybe it's something much bigger, like putting off launching a business or pursuing a new idea. You might feel like you need to read one more book or take one more course to be ready. The truth is, no matter what you're procrastinating, you're probably not making it any better by waiting around. Sometimes, the best thing you can do is act.

I've found that identifying the reason for our procrastination can help us avoid the pitfalls.

Here are five reasons you may be procrastinating:

1. **You lose motivation.**
It's easy to have motivation when you're first launching your business. You create your LLC, buy your domain, create a logo, build a website, create your social media pag-

es, and tell your friends about what you're doing, but then things don't happen as quickly as you'd like for them to. This may cause you to lose motivation, and your dream may start to feel more like a job. Plus, as an entrepreneur, you don't have a boss looking over your shoulder and giving you deadlines. You might start putting off the things you know you need to do because the work doesn't feel fun anymore, even though you know your business will suffer because of it. Why do we do this to ourselves?

In business and life, motivation will ebb and flow. You have to instead focus on your goal, the result, and know there will be many ups and downs until you get there. You can't wait for motivation; you have to take action.

2. You are operating off of emotion.

Sometimes, we procrastinate because we're going off of our emotions. We're tired, discouraged, or fearful. As an entrepreneur, if you work off the way you feel, you will lose. No one wakes up every day wanting to dive right into work, but successful entrepreneurs do it anyway. Their goal is more important than how they feel at the moment. Feelings are temporary, but goals are permanent. I encourage you to find something that will get you in the right state of mind. Listen to your favorite music, a motivational podcast, or read a devotional. Find whatever it is for you, and start your day with it.

4. You don't know where to start.

I often work with clients who procrastinate because they don't know where to start. They often work alone, and the list of things they must do feels a mile long. That overwhelmed feeling causes people to feel stuck, and as a result, they do nothing. If you find yourself feeling overwhelmed, make a list of everything you need to do, then prioritize the list in order of importance. You can't do everything at once, so this will make you feel more organized. Break down the things you will accomplish this week, then break that list into the three things you will do each day. Suddenly, your list doesn't seem as overwhelming, and you won't feel the need to procrastinate. It's good to reward yourself for small tasks you accomplish along the way. For example, if you go to the gym five times a week, reward yourself with a cheat meal at your favorite restaurant on Saturday. This practice creates an incentive for checking things off your list.

4. You don't know what to do.
Sometimes, you may be unsure of what steps you need to take to get to your goal. Are we doing the right things? Should we start a podcast, write weekly blog posts, or spend that time cold-calling to get leads? There's no one answer for every business, but I do know that imperfect action is better than no action at all. Just start and evaluate what you're doing every 30 days to see what brings you the most success. Once you can identify what's working best for you, hone in on it. In business and marketing, we're constantly testing new things to see what will work. It's the only way!

If you're still feeling stuck, a business coach or mentor can help you put your priorities in place and tackle the things you need to do first. If you don't have access to a coach or a mentor, find someone you admire in your industry and do what they do. There's no reason to reinvent the wheel. If someone you admire is having success, emulate what they did to get there, but put your spin on it
.

5. You are scared to fail.
When you start something new, there's always a chance you might fail. Despite this reality, you can't go into business being afraid to fail. Failure in some aspects is inevitable. It's about learning from your failures and getting better.

No successful entrepreneur has gone without failing. Maybe their business was an overall success, but not everything they tried along the way worked. We often launch new marketing initiatives to test them before recommending them to our clients. Some work, some fail! It's part of the business. We don't dwell on the failures; we learn from them and move on. You should constantly test new things to see what works best and then go all in when you see it hit.

This is the reason your "why" is so important. You have to remind yourself why you're doing what you're doing and remember your end goal.

We all fail – even the most successful entrepreneurs. The difference is that they didn't dwell on it. They picked themselves up, learned from the failure and tried again.

You need to remember that you're in control of your momentum. Put a plan together that you can follow, stick with it, and see the success that starts to stack up in your life.

Things That Get in the Way of Your Success, #9

Being Lazy: 10 Ways to Beat Laziness & Be Productive!

One time, I met with a client who told me she wasn't happy with where she was in her life. She felt bored with her job, unhappy with her weight, dissatisfied with her marriage, and distant from her kids as they were getting older.

During our meeting, we started to break down each area of her life that she was unhappy with and make a plan to get her out of her rut. As we started to go over each area and listed the things she could do to improve her situation, it became clear that she didn't actually want to change. Why? Because making changes can be really hard! It can feel overwhelming and even impossible to make big changes in your life, especially if you've been living a certain way for a long time, and it's very tempting to be lazy and complacent.

I told her that if she really wanted her life to improve, she couldn't be complacent and unwilling to change. I realized from talking to her, however, that the idea of making several big changes at once was too daunting. Instead of tackling everything at once, we decided she would start with the easiest area to change first (her career). We set goals and came up with actionable items she would do each week to accomplish those goals.

There are small, disciplined things you can do everyday that will increase your productivity. Sometimes, making small, incremental changes over time will be more fruitful in the long run than making drastic ones. Once you make a new good habit in one area of your life, that work ethic will spill over into every other area.

I came up with 10 ways to be more productive and avoid laziness:

1. Put your alarm clock across the room so you have to get up and turn it off each day. This practice will help you avoid the snooze button, since you'll already be out of bed. If you start your day snoozing, you're setting yourself up for an unproductive day. When you get up ready to face the day, you'll find that you accomplish your personal and professional goals faster.

2. Keep your personal environment clean. Studies show that maintaining a clean work environment increases productivity. Having a clean, organized place to do your work will make you feel more put together and also sends a clear message to anyone who works with you that they are to take you seriously. The same goes for your environment at home: if you're coming home to a mess, you won't be able to fully relax and take care of yourself. You need that time at home to help you recharge, and you can't do that if your home is a mess.

3. If you want to be healthier, surround yourself with nutritious food choices. You're much more likely to eat healthy when there are no bad options available. Set aside time to meal prep each week so you have healthy meals planned out for the week. If you know you're usually tired when you get home from work and aren't in the mood to cook, plan ahead and have your meals already cooked or subscribe to a healthy food delivery service.

4. Set mini goals each week and reward yourself when you hit them. Maybe it's going to the gym three times a week or making five sales calls per day. At the end of the week, reward yourself with a cheat meal or go get your nails done! Do something that makes you feel celebrated for your hard work.

5. Limit your TV time. It's easy to get sucked into hours and hours of Netflix, but remember that time spent watching TV can also be used for other things that get you closer to your goals, like working out, cleaning or spending time with family. Give yourself one night a week where you watch your favorite show. Treat it as a reward so the other areas of your life get the attention they deserve.

6. Find people who motivate you. It's hard to reach your goals when your friends' goals aren't aligned with yours. Find friends with similar goals as yours, and pour into them. For example, I have friends I work out with every morning who hold me accountable and keep me focused on my fitness goals.

7. Listen to motivational podcasts. There are so many great podcasts out there, you're guaranteed to find one you like. Listening to someone inspiring every day can help you kick start your day. If you want to learn from some amazing women CEOs and entrepreneurs, I host the DO IT MY WAY Podcast, empowering women to do life on their terms with no regrets, hesitation or fear. Check it out anywhere you watch/listen to your podcasts or at DoItMyWayPodcast.com.

8. Tackle the big things on your list first. I always try to identify three big things I need to accomplish that day before I do anything else. That way if I get busy and don't get to the rest, I know I still accomplished the three most important things. It gives you a sense of pride to set these small goals every day and reach them.

9. Get enough sleep. If you get an adequate amount of sleep each night, you won't be sluggish and tired as you accomplish your goals during the day. Make sure your room is a peaceful, clean place to relax at night, allowing you to forget the worries of the day and get quality sleep.

10. Be conscious of your social media scrolling. Don't get trapped spending hours of your day on social media. Set specific times to check it (like morning, noon and right before bed) and set a timer to only scroll for 10 minutes. That way you'll stay up-to-date with what's happening in the world, but you won't waste time mindlessly scrolling.

Remember: the small, disciplined things you do each day will create massive momentum in your life!

Things That Get in the Way of Your Success, #10

Fear: The Three Biggest Fears Women CEOs & Entrepreneurs Face.

Coaching women CEOs and entrepreneurs lights me on fire. I relate to the struggles they often face. Whether it's working hard to prove themselves in male-dominated spaces, or the fear that comes with starting their own business ventures. The truth is, there is no one more efficient with their time than a mom who's running a household and a business – these are the women who inspire me every day.

But at the end of the day, we're human, and fear often holds us back from making big moves. I see it all the time: A woman entrepreneur with a great idea and amazing potential but she's scared of failure. She's worried she won't have enough time to be a successful wife, mom and entrepreneur, and she's overly concerned with what other people think. Fear is truly the biggest thing that holds people back from accomplishing their goals.

These are the top three fears I see in women entrepreneurs and my advice for how to conquer them:

1. Self-doubt. We've all been there: you have a great idea and are excited to tell someone about it, but their reaction isn't what you expected. They might bring up all of the things that could potentially go wrong and deflate your confidence. You tell yourself, 'Maybe they're right – can I really do this? Is this really a good idea?' My advice? Go with your gut! I remember a business coach once told me that starting a niche website for moms was a bad idea, but my intuition said differently, and I had a feeling it would succeed. As a mom, I wanted to connect with other moms online. I knew advertisers would want to sell to the prime audience of women, aged 25 to 54. I ignored their negativity and went with my gut, using their doubt to fuel me. On many late nights, however, the negative voice crept back into my mind. Was he right after all? Was I wasting my time and energy? But I didn't give in to self-doubt – I was on a mission, and I wasn't going to let anyone stop me from doing it my way!

2. Time. Many women are afraid they don't have enough time to succeed. Balancing kids, family, home, business, friends and other commitments can make it seem like you have no spare time to pursue anything else. Women tend to feel afraid to commit to a business because they're afraid other areas of their life will suffer. But the truth is, we all have time for what's important to us! Is starting a business important to you? Will it give you more financial freedom? Will it help your family? What would your life look like if you didn't have to worry about money and you could hire people to help you do the busy work at home and in your business? With the extra time, could you be a better wife, mom or friend? What would it do for your business if you only did what you were great at and delegated all of the other tasks? You have to identify your why – why you want to start your business – and remind yourself of it every day. Then, you'll need to adjust your schedule and only do the things that are most important to you!

3. Ego. As women, we have a tendency to feel like we have to please everyone. It's important, however, that you stop spending your time trying to appease or impress others. You'll waste time, money and energy trying to get people whose opinions aren't important to say you're great. As far as social media goes, it's easy to get caught in the trap of endless scrolling or stressing over likes and comments. I run an online digital agency, so social media is how we make money. I've been in the social media trap before, and it's just not worth it. People often ask if I saw this or that on social media, and most of the time, my answer to them is 'No.' Sure, I post and put content out, but I try to not spend my time scrolling through Facebook, Instagram or TikTok. I have million dollar goals I'm trying to reach, and spending my time browsing social media isn't going to help me get there. I have clients who spend hours stressing over which picture they should post on their social media, but in my opinion, it's not worth the energy spent stressing over something just to see if it will get likes. Put your ego to the side, post what you want to post, and people will respond to it. It's hard not to care what people think of you, especially on social media, but you have to remind yourself that it's not the most important thing and that you have bigger goals to reach.

Is fear holding you back? Is it getting in the way of you pitching to a big client, or going after a major investor? Fear is a story we make up in our heads. Try telling yourself a new story – one that shows you as a confident, successful entrepreneur living her best life.

Things That Get in the Way of Your Success, #11

Burn Out: Feeling Burned Out? 5 Ways to Recharge

Being a high-level CEO or entrepreneur can be a grind. Day after day, you must commit to doing the small, disciplined things that will take you to the next level. The daily grind isn't always glamorous, and it can take years before you succeed. In addition to keeping up with the demands of your business, you may have kids to take care of, a spouse who needs you, commitments to friends, neighbors, or your church you need to keep. And yet, the to-do list for your job isn't getting any smaller. It can lead to downright burnout, which makes everything in your life seem complex - even simple tasks like getting out of bed in the morning.

Burnout is a real thing. No one is at the finish line cheering you on. You're often alone on an island, working hard to make your dream come true.

When you're an entrepreneur, you are your motivator. No one is making you get to the office early or work on the weekends. Yet, you find yourself going above and beyond because there are a million things to do, and the only option is to succeed.

Not to mention that if you have a team, you probably feel enormous pressure to hit your revenue goals so you can make your payroll each month.

I've been in this exact position. Being your own boss can be highly stressful, and it's easy to burn out when working 12-hour days with no gratification. No one is patting you on the back for putting in the work, and on top of the stress, working long hours may create tension at home with your family and spouse.

Even if you haven't reached your goals yet, you still need to take time to recharge each week so you can avoid burnout and keep working hard. Remember: you must take care of yourself along the ride, or you'll never reach your destination.

Here are five ways I've learned to recharge over the years:

1. **Get seven to eight hours of sleep every night.** I didn't always do this, and I know it may seem impossible for you now. The reality is the work you must do will still be there in the morning. Do what you HAVE to do each day first, so the secondary work is last and can be put off till tomorrow if necessary. Studies show your brain and body only recover adequately from the day if you get seven to eight hours of sleep per night. I'm religious about my sleep time, as I mentioned earlier in the book. I'm in bed by 9 pm and up at 4:30 am daily. I try to stick to this schedule on the weekends, too, give or take an hour. When I stick to this schedule, I find that my brain is sharper, my body feels more rested, and I start the day peacefully. You don't have to be a morning person; maybe you are better at night. Adjust the time to fit your lifestyle.

2. **Create a peaceful place in your home.** My zen spot is our backyard. After work, I come home, leave my phone alone for a few hours, chat with my kids about their days,

cook dinner, and connect with my husband. When the weather is nice, we like to cook dinner, eat outside, listen to music and get in the hot tub before bed - it's a great way to unwind and recharge my battery for the day. If I've had a difficult day and I make it home before everyone else, I like to sit in the backyard in silence, take deep breaths, and listen to the sounds of nature. I let all the negative thoughts of the day leave my mind and body, so when everyone is home, I'm a more upbeat version of myself. Your peaceful place might be a local park or even your bedroom; make sure it's somewhere you can escape for a little while.

3. Move your body! It may seem counterproductive to move your body to recharge or relax. Still, exercise reduces levels of the body's stress hormones and stimulates the production of endorphins (chemicals in the brain that act as the body's natural painkillers and mood elevators). It's hard for me to unwind and take a break from the thousands of thoughts that seem to be swirling around in my head, but I find that when I get out of my mind and into my body, I never regret it. If you don't have time for an hour-long, intense class at the gym, try walking a mile around your neighborhood or doing a 15-minute yoga class on YouTube. My daughter is a junior in college, and my favorite time of the day is our daily walks. She lives two hours away, but we walk and talk on the phone. It's a way for us to both get our exercise in and vent about our days. I wouldn't trade this quality time for anything!

4. Change up your environment. Changing your physical location gives you a new perspective in life. For example, if you're working from home every day and having difficulty getting motivated, change it up. Go work at a local coffee shop or cafe - getting dressed and getting out of the house will instantly make you feel more motivated. If you have the opportunity to travel, I highly encourage you to go someplace that inspires you. It doesn't even have to be out of state or country. Taking a weekend trip to a new city can help you get a fresh perspective and recharge. For me, a bonus of taking a little time off is that I usually come back with a new business idea. I know a lot of entrepreneurs who haven't taken a vacation in years because they think their businesses will suffer, but that's untrue. What will hurt your business is the effects of burnout you could face if you don't build in break and recharge time. Schedule a vacation at least once a year, even if it's a mini staycation at home with your phone on Do Not Disturb mode!

5. Make time for friends and family. Life isn't just about work. I've had many years where work is what I thought about the majority of the time, but I've learned to work hard during a specific time frame so I can play hard, too. Set hours when you work and leave all other distractions to the side, and then have particular friends and family time when you set work aside. I work hard during the day, and then once I get home, it's all about my family. I try to always make time for friends, too, whether planning a dinner or even a girl's trip. In my opinion, maintaining solid friendships is an integral part of being a successful adult.

Think back to your last vacation or the last time you spent some quality alone time. How did it make you feel? Start to notice your body and mind and the things you do throughout your life that enable you to recharge. There's no right or wrong answer; it's all about what makes you feel like the best, most capable version of yourself. Find things that bring you inner peace and let you forget the stress of life so you can properly recharge.

Things That Get in the Way of Your Success, #12

Lack of a Schedule: You Have to Schedule Everything!

In business, as well as in life, everything needs to be on the calendar.

This concept seems simple, but a problem so many entrepreneurs struggle with is scheduling. It's challenging but essential to set aside dedicated time for personal development, your kids' events, quality time with your partner, and even personal care appointments, like visiting the doctor or getting your hair done.

One of my clients is a successful entrepreneur in the medical industry who struggled greatly with scheduling. He described how he felt as being similar to a hamster on a wheel, going around and around but getting nowhere. He felt like he was flying by the seat of his pants each day, rushing from patient to patient but neglecting many of the obligations he had in his personal life. Many of the things he said he wanted to happen weren't happening because he didn't schedule them. For example, he wanted to make it a goal to exercise daily but failed because he didn't schedule it, and he let other things get in the way. As a result, he felt sluggish and tired and wasn't the best version of himself. After he decided to make exercise a priority, however, he scheduled workout sessions very early each morning before the workday began so that nothing could distract him. All he needed to realize was that taking care of himself was just as important as an appointment with a patient and that his personal time deserved the same level of scheduling as his work obligations.

When you're an entrepreneur, there isn't anyone making you clock in at 8:00 a.m. and out at 5:00 p.m. Your schedule is entirely up to you, which is a beautiful thing, but too much freedom can be detrimental. It would help if you made a schedule that works for you and your lifestyle, or nothing will ever get accomplished. A schedule makes you feel in control of your environment. If you protect your time and schedule everything important to you, your personal and professional life will reap the benefits.

Make time for the things that are important to you and stick to it. Most people make a schedule for their work obligations but neglect scheduling their personal lives, which leaves them feeling unfulfilled and like they're coming up short. If you schedule everything, you will feel in control of your day, allowing you to dedicate time and effort to each item on your list. Plus, this schedule allows you to spend a lot of quality time with my family after work, which is so important. It's all about identifying what your personal and professional priorities are, creating the right routine, and sticking to it.

My Google calendar is truly my best friend. Every single thing I do is on the calendar, whether it's work appointments, deadlines, nail appointments, or even Saturday yoga with my mom - it's all there. If I don't put it in the calendar, it's not getting done. I encourage anyone to use Google calendar, because it syncs up with your phone and gives you reminders when you have tasks coming up. Having a digital calendar in our day in age is so important, and allows you to be flexible. Even when you're not at the office, you can access the calendar on your phone and make changes on the fly. My team also has access to my calendar so they know where I am and when not to bother me.

I always try to treat my personal care and personal development appointments just like I would an appointment with my number one clients - they are non-negotiable and are equally important! If you don't dedicate time to take care of yourself, you won't be able to show up and do your best each day for your team, clients or customers.

The phrase "I just don't have enough hours in my day" really isn't true. A great exercise to do is map out your day and record where your time is really being spent. Once you write everything down, decide which items are important for you to do and which can be delegated to a team member. Look at where you're overcommitting and under-committing your time and make adjustments.

Which areas are you failing in because you haven't properly scheduled your time? Maybe it's a relationship, your nutrition, or wanting to learn a new professional skill. The most successful entrepreneurs I coach schedule out everything in their lives and stick to it.

Here are my seven best scheduling tips:

1. Understand what you can realistically achieve with your time each day and schedule it accordingly.
2. Make sure you have enough time for essential tasks. If you don't, you may need to re-prioritize your time or get up earlier.
3. Add contingency time for the unexpected.
4. Avoid taking on more than you can handle.

'No' is a powerful word.

5. Schedule things you have to do daily to reach your financial and business goals. These are the non-negotiables.
6. Have enough time for family, friends, exercise and hobbies - these are just as important as work!
7. Achieve a good work-life balance.

Time is the one resource we can't buy, but we often waste it or use it ineffectively. Scheduling helps you think about what you want to achieve in a day, week or month and it keeps you on track to accomplish your goals. You've got this!

Things That Get in the Way of Your Success, #13

Lack of Emotional Intelligence: How Your EI Affects Your Business

Emotional intelligence is vital to running a successful business. Emotions have an effect on your team, customers, relationships and employee retention.

Your emotional quotient (EQ) is the ability to manage your emotions and the emotions of others. Do you fly off the handle when a team member upsets you or a client does something that makes you really mad? Lacking control of your emotions is a good way to quickly lose team members or clients.
I've seen entrepreneurs ruin their business because they lacked emotional intelligence. They lash out and overreact at their team members' actions, making it difficult to retain them long-term. The overly-emotional approach never works. You won't motivate your team to work harder by tearing into them, but you can empower them by being a great leader.

Here are some of the pillars of emotional intelligence:

1. **Self-awareness** - It's crucial to recognize your emotions and the effects they have. Do you get upset easily? Are you hot-tempered? Do you cry often? It's good to know

these things about yourself, so you can recognize when your emotions are starting to get out of control. When you know your emotional tendencies, you can take steps to remove yourself from a situation or calm yourself down, so your emotions don't have a negative impact on your friends, family or team members.

2. **Self-regulation** - You need to be able to control your emotions. This is thinking before you act, avoiding flying off the handle, verbally attacking, or firing off a rude email when emotions are high. You have to learn to take a step back and evaluate the situation to understand the other person's point of view and how your actions will affect your company. Avoid making rash, emotional decisions. Remaining calm can be the most powerful trait of a successful entrepreneur.
Internal motivation - People with a high EQ are self-motivated. They pursue personal goals for reasons of self-development and self-gratification, rather than for money, titles, external praise or esteem. If you don't have a strong sense of internal motivation, entrepreneurship may not be for you. You have to be a self-starter to put in the work even when you don't feel like it.

3. **Empathy** - Empathy is the degree to which you can empathize with other people's emotions and understand the viewpoints of others. I highly recommend having each team member take the DISC profile and the Enneagram to understand their personality type. This way, you can make sure they're in a role that will bring them and the organization success. Empathy is definitely a daily practice and involves listening to your team just as much as you talk to them.

4. **Social skills** - Leaders communicate effectively and are good at identifying and resolving conflicts. They also inspire others by leading by example and giving praise to others when earned. Using their emotional intelligence,

they easily build trust and respect with others and are good at managing relationships and building networks. A good leader will constantly communicate with their team to get feedback and ideas from them, so they can always be improving.

Here's a list of traits of successful leaders who have a high EQ:

- They are better at staying calm under pressure.
- They listen as often or more often than they speak.
- They lead by example.
- They make thoughtful business decisions.
- They take criticism well, admitting to their mistakes and learning from them.
- They keep their emotions in check and can discuss tough issues maturely.
- They can effectively resolve conflict.
- They are empathetic to team members.

In order to improve your emotional intelligence, start incorporating these practices into your daily life.

Pause before you speak, act, or respond. This will help you calm down and think through what the best solution is for everyone involved, all while keeping your emotions in check. I have learned this over the years. I have plenty of moments where I spoke too soon and then regretted it later. It is always best to pause and think before you act!

Listen to those around you. Listening will help you understand the emotional needs of others. It takes the focus off of you and gives you a clear view of what the people around you need from you. I have to remind myself to do this daily.

Attempt to control your thoughts. We can't control what happens to us or the emotions we feel in a moment, but we can control how we respond to them by reframing our thoughts. Instead of blaming yourself or someone else when something negative happens, think about why they may have acted that way and what the best, most thoughtful way to respond is.

Praise others. Lifting up other people trains your brain to focus on the good in others, encouraging empathy and allowing a deeper understanding of other people's needs and motivations. Using praise and positivity can also help you have constructive discussions on tough issues, because it decreases defensiveness and encourages openness. If I'm getting frustrated at work, I will often sit back and think of all of the GREAT things my team is doing. I'll randomly send each one of them an email thanking them for what they do for D2 every day, which brings my mindset back to a positive state.

Be able to take criticism. It can be hurtful, but it can also be helpful, as it opens us up to outside perspectives. In the face of criticism, ask yourself - How can I improve and grow from this? I have started having my team answer these questions at the end of every year so I can get real feedback from them:

1. What is one thing you are grateful for right now?
2. What is working really well for you right now?
3. What is exciting you right now?
4. What are you struggling with right now?
5. What do you need my help with right now?

This is a great way to get real feedback. Most of the time, the team answers it with work related answers, but every once in a while, someone will answer with something personal that I had no idea was going on. It also allows me to get real feedback on how I'm doing and if they need my help.

Pay attention to body language. Most communication is non-verbal. If you only listen with your ears, you could be missing out on how a person really feels. This is a really great tip in sales. If you can read sales cues on how the prospect is feeling, you will know when to go for the close! If they are sitting back with their arms crossed, they are skeptical. If they are leaning in toward you, they are interested!

Apologize. Intentions get misunderstood and feelings get hurt regularly. Apologizing shows compassion and encourages us to better understand one another while building trust and respect. The quicker you learn to own up to your mistakes with your team and with clients, the better your life will be! We are all human!

Try to see from another person's point of view. When in a disagreement, consider the needs, motivations, and emotions that may be shaping another's priorities and opinions. Ask the reasons behind their thoughts and try to genuinely understand them. I have team members who are Enneagram 1's, which is a perfectionist and very detail oriented, basically, my opposite! They make decisions slowly and like to think everything out in great detail before they act. They also spend hours and hours doing smaller tasks because they want it to be perfect. This is a challenging personality for me to manage, but think of how I am to them! I am an Enneagram 3 who is very goal oriented and likes to move fast! I am always pushing them beyond their comfort zone, which I have to step back sometimes and see it from their point of view. I used to just get extremely frustrated with them, but now I know how they work, so I have adjusted how I interact with them. I also hired a project manager to be a "buffer" between us who has way more patience than me and it has turned out beautifully!

Communicate your feelings. When you are offended or upset, communicate to the offending party in a calm, non-threatening way so everyone can gain a mutual understanding and avoid future problems. The way I have to do this is address the situation the next day. If something happens that I am upset about, I need to step back, give it a day and calmly come back to it. Sometimes I am better writing it out in an email and then asking the person for a meeting to discuss it once I have carefully crafted my thoughts. This has served me very well but I had to learn it the hard way.

Things That Get in the Way of Your Success, #14

Always Playing Defense: Are You Playing Offense or Defense in your Business?

Recently, I had a meeting with a client to discuss their company's progress over the last year. They're a start-up company in the stages of trying to secure funding, but they aren't having any luck. The founder is involved in several other businesses so he only dedicates a few hours each week to the start-up. I finally had to have a heart-to-heart discussion when he was frustrated that things hadn't moved along faster.

What I told him was simple: He was playing defense in his business rather than offense. He was doing busy work waiting for something to happen, rather than taking initiative and creating his own momentum. I asked him what he'd done in his business in the last week that was proactive instead of waiting for people to get back to him. Waiting is defense – you have to create an offense in your business to get things moving. You won't score without an offense.

Offensive moves are growing, marketing, hiring and trying new things, while defensive moves are waiting for people to call you instead of reaching out to them first, being reactive and playing it safe.

An offensive player in business works on tasks that get them closer to scoring, and delegates other tasks that get in the way of them reaching their goal. They ignore distractions and keep their eyes on the prize. A defensive player lacks momentum because they're always reacting, which often leads to burnout.

Let's talk about offense versus defense in your life.

Do you know friends who complain about being out of shape who do nothing to change it? They're playing defense by complaining about the current state of their body instead of playing offense, which would require them to work out and stick to a meal plan.

Playing offense is about trying new things to see what works so that you have a chance to get what you really want in life. While failure is a real possibility, you at least know you're trying and will probably get to your goal faster than you would if you were just waiting around, maintaining the status quo, resisting change, and keeping things the way they are.

Let's talk about your clients for a minute. Do you play offense and get ahead of problems before they come up, or do you wait until your client complains and then scramble to come up with a solution? If you're playing offense, then you're in the driver's seat of both your business and your life.

Here are some of my best tips for operating an offensive:

1. **Create a schedule and stick to it**. There's no better offense than a planned-out day. Make a list of all of the small things you need to do that day to get you closer to your goals and check them off. Proactively planning out what you need to do every day is playing offense.

2. Disable social media, email and phone notifications while you're working on your offense. Distractions will take you away from making the impact you want to make.

3. Remember that playing offense doesn't mean you'll always score. You might not score all the time, but the small steps you take every day will get you closer to your end goal.

4. Surround yourself with people who are also playing offense. You are who you surround yourself with, so surround yourself with people who are actively trying to make their lives better! If your circle isn't pushing you to be your best, it's time to get a new circle.

Of course, you have to find a balance in business and in life. Even though you may try to play offense every day, there will still be unforeseen things that happen that force you to play defense when they hit. The most important thing you can do is focus on what you can control. Start your day on an offensive note by working out, reading or listening to something positive. Make a list of the three big things you will accomplish that day and do them.

Remember, you will never score if you don't set up an offense!

Things That Get in the Way of Your Success, #15

Fear of Doing Hard Things: Want to Succeed? Do Hard Things!

I spend a lot of time coaching entrepreneurs whose businesses aren't where they want them to be. What I've found is, oftentimes, these entrepreneurs want to be successful but aren't willing to do the hard things to get there.

We see people like Sara Blakely, the founder of Spanx, who is now a billionaire – she makes it look so easy! But her path to success wasn't easy. She did hard things to get to where she is today. Sara found a problem that wasn't addressed in her industry and solved it by creating women's undergarments that sucked you in and didn't show through your clothes. Over the course of 14 years, she created a billion-dollar company and set an example that many other women entrepreneurs have followed since. I wonder how many people had a great idea like Sara did, but weren't willing to grind for 14 years? She chose to do all of the hard things and it paid off.

Sara used $5,000 in savings that she'd earned from her job selling fax machines door-to-door to start her brand in 2000. Over a decade later, her company was earning 20% profit margins on nearly $250 million in annual sales. In October

2021, Sara sold a majority stake in Spanx to a private equity firm with a deal that valued Spanx at $1.2 billion. She sold 80% of the company, meaning she accepted a $960 million cash-out. Not a bad outcome after a $5,000 investment!

We all want to start a business and watch the money roll in, but that doesn't happen day one. I coach my clients to do the hard things first so they can create a proven process that takes their business to the next level. You have to put in the hard work and long hours before you can see the fruits of your labor.

In order to have a successful business, you have to have success in other areas of your life as well. If you aren't happy in your personal life, chances are that unhappiness will spill over into your professional life. The goal is to be your best at work and at home. Many people have the personal goal of getting into better shape, but as you get older it becomes much more difficult. The good news, however, is that it is possible – you just have to do hard things to get there. It takes a lot of discipline to commit to a healthy lifestyle and say 'no' to bad habits. If you choose the healthy path, your body will change, your mind will become more clear and you'll get stronger. But it takes doing hard things to get there.

You should never stop trying to do hard things. I try to put myself in an uncomfortable situation physically, mentally or at work often so I can continuously improve myself. Last year I started taking challenging hot yoga classes once a week that pushed my body to the limit. These classes are super intense, but I feel so amazing afterwards. At work, I'm committing to doing a podcast interview once a month with a high level female CEO or entrepreneur. Being on camera is an uncomfortable thing for me, but it's a great exercise in being brave and putting myself out there. And it's paid off as I have connected with so many inspiring women who have sent referrals my way or became a client! When you do something hard, you grow. That's why I'll never stop doing hard things! This book was a big goal of mine and one I thought I would never finish, but here I am a published author! And for the record, it was way harder than I thought!

Doing hard things is what will separate you from everyone else. Do you want to make more money? Make time to do the hard things and do them every day. Do you want to lose weight? You know what to do – create healthy habits and stick to them. Pretty soon they will become a part of your routine and you'll start to see amazing benefits from doing hard things.

Here are some of my biggest pointers for doing the hard things:

- Get to the office a little bit earlier than you usually do. Use this time for personal development, planning and reading up on the latest trends in your industry.
- Make sales calls every day, even when you don't feel like it.
- Solve customer service complaints and learn from them.
- Move your body every day.
- Meal-prep healthy meals so you don't make bad choices and lose momentum in your work day.
- Say 'no' to sugar and processed foods.
- Let go of the employee who doesn't contribute to your company's culture.
- Distance yourself from negative people in your life who don't support your goals.
- Drink your bodyweight in ounces of water each day.
- Forgive that person that hurt you.

What are you going to add to your personal and professional life that is hard? Adding some challenges to your personal and professional life will only make you stronger. Do something hard every day and you will succeed at whatever goals you set out to reach!

Things That Get in the Way of Your Success, #16

Taking Everything Personally: Why do We Always Take it Personal?

In business, people always say, "Don't take it personally, it's just business." Well, that's easier said than done. It's hard not to take things personally when you put your heart and soul into your business. When you've spent 12-hour days getting your business off the ground, or pouring yourself into a client, everything feels personal.

The truth is, no one cares about your business as much as you do. And it's not through any fault of their own – the reality is, everyone you know is the center of their own world. They're too focused on themselves and their dealings to care about yours as much as you do.

Here are a few more harsh truths that you may encounter as an entrepreneur:

Someone is going to copy your business.
Whether it's in their social media posts, sales pitches or websites, someone (and probably more than one) is going to copy what you're doing. The first time this happened to me, I dis-

covered that a peer of mine who owned a marketing agency copied the exact wording we use on our website and in sales pitches to go after clients. They weren't a digital agency and weren't knowledgeable about digital marketing, so I'd shared with them my strategy they should be doing if they wanted to survive in the digital age. It stung, and I felt betrayed. Later, however, I took a step back and realized that even though my feelings were hurt, there are enough clients to go around for all of us, and if I helped them keep their employees on the payroll, then I succeeded.

A client will unexpectedly quit.

It might even be your best client who you've done incredible work for or the one who praised you a couple of months before, crediting you for their entire success.

I'll never forget getting an email from a client saying they were canceling. It happened to be a client I considered a friend, too. I'd shared so much free advice with them over the years, helped them with their start-up, and eventually became their agency for their new idea. We helped them with the entire concept: the logo, website, videos and their digital campaign. They had so much success right out of the gate and started making money right away, which they credited to us. Two months later, I got an email saying they wanted to cancel. I was so hurt and couldn't understand their reasoning. Worse, they didn't even give me the decency of a phone call or in-person meeting to explain.

The more I thought about the situation, I realized that the one thing I couldn't control or understand is their finances. Maybe they were in over their heads or spent more than they were making, which is easy to do. It was hurtful and hard to understand, but they're human and humans will disappoint you when you least expect it. It took me several days to get over my disappointment, but I decided I was thankful to have the opportunity to help them grow and for the amazing testimonial I now had to share with other clients.

An employee who you've poured money and time into will quit.
This is an inevitable part of owning a business. People are people, and ultimately, they're looking out for themselves. Most jobs are a stepping stone to get someone to the career they ultimately want to have. It can hurt to think about all of the time and energy you poured into that person, but that's life. They're a better person for it and your company is better because of the work they did. Very few jobs last forever, so you have to be thankful for the time they dedicated to you.

You will have a client who gets content and doesn't care to scale and grow.
As an Enneagram Type 3, this concept is so hard for me to understand! I've pitched people marketing ideas before who've told me they don't need any more customers. To me, that doesn't make sense. Do you think Amazon sits around and thinks, "We have enough customers, let's hang it up."? No way! They scale, grow and take over the world.

But you have to remember that not everyone has the same goals as you, and they might see their business from a different perspective. That's OK – meet them where they are and help them live the life they want to live.

You will have someone leave you a bad Google review.
It doesn't matter how great your company or customer service is, someone will leave you a bad Google review. In ten years of owning D2, I've had two bad Google reviews. One was from a client who couldn't pay his bill, so I canceled his services. The other was a client who I hadn't worked with in four years, who left a review saying he was dissatisfied, even though by all accounts, everything went great while we worked together and he never expressed any unhappiness.

It's pretty much inevitable that you'll get a bad Google review. How you respond to it will be what your customers look for. Taking things personally and leading with your emotions will get in the way of your success. Not everyone will like you or your company, and that's OK. You don't need to be all things to everyone, and that would be exhausting anyway!

If you find yourself taking things personally, take a deep breath. Ask yourself if you will care about what's bothering you in one month or one year. Take a step back when you find yourself getting defensive, heated or hurt over a business situation. Realize it isn't about you – it's a business decision, just like the ones you make daily to do what's best for you and your business. Grow and learn from the experience. As a leader, your team is looking at you during times of adversity way more closely than they look at you during times of success.

Things That Get in the Way of Your Success, #17

Fear of Taking Action: Quit Talking About it, Do it!

I'm blessed to coach entrepreneurs of all races, backgrounds and economic statuses from all over the country. Each of my clients brings to the table his or her unique perspective and preconceived notions, based on how they grew up. Some clients have a poverty mindset that they have to overcome, while others lack faith in themselves due to the stories they were told as kids that they still believe to be true (i.e. "You'll never be good enough," or "That's a dumb idea," etc.).

Nothing is more satisfying than bringing these entrepreneurs together through group coaching and creating an environment where everyone understands each others' fears and where they come from. They lean on each other, pray for each other, cheer each other on and offer each other an amazing support system. The truth is, entrepreneurship can be a very lonely job, especially if you're a solopreneur in the beginning. It's hard because you don't have anyone to bounce ideas off of or to tell you that what you're doing isn't working and you need to pivot.

I feel like God has called me to be that person for the entrepreneurs I coach – the person to help steer them in the right direction and provide unbiased advice. I'm able to see things they don't in their business and guide them along a path to success, no matter what their goals are.

All of the entrepreneurs I work with are different and face unique challenges in their lives and businesses, but they all have one thing in common: They are action-takers. These are the people who really act instead of just talking about what they're going to do. They may not always have the right answer, but in my opinion, imperfect action is better than no action at all.

I'm part of a personal branding coaching program and we vet the entrepreneurs who are interested to see if they're a good fit for the program. One of the very first things I look for is whether or not someone is an action-taker. Has this person spent 20 years thinking of their business idea without taking action, or have they taken imperfect action along the way to see what works?

Recently, I had an inspiring phone call with a potential personal branding academy member. She was a 26-year-old former Division I soccer player who became a personal trainer and nutrition coach. At the time, she was working at a gym making $15 an hour and living in a crowded house with her family that was taking a toll on her mental health. Her car was falling apart and she had very little money to spare at that moment, but she knew that she wanted to make a big change in her career and in her life. Despite not having a lot of spending money and not knowing how she was going to pay for it, she was so excited to join our personal branding academy because she knew she had to take serious action to turn her life around. I knew at that moment that she would be successful.

The way that she took action and made a big commitment by joining our program lit a fire under her to succeed. She already had so much internal drive and passion, and by joining our academy, we gave her all of the personal branding tools she needed. Now, don't get me wrong, I'm not telling you to go into debt or spend money you don't have, but sometimes you have to take a risk to succeed. If that client hadn't taken action, she would probably be in the same situation two years from now.

I've always been an action-taker and when I made the decision to commit to my new career path, a fire was lit under me. It was incredibly scary to leave my stable job (and six-figure salary) in television behind to become an entrepreneur. I knew once I took action and committed, it was sink or swim. At the time, I was the breadwinner in my family and we were in the middle of building our dream home. The only way we qualified for the loan was by using both of our salaries, and I had just left mine behind. This meant there was no time for sleeping in and no time for slacking off – I had to make money, and make it quickly. I have since realized that I thrive in that environment. Sometimes putting yourself in situations where you have no choice but to succeed is where you operate in your genius!

What in your life do you need to take action on? Is there something you've been thinking about for years but never started? Maybe it was starting a business or starting a weight loss journey or even creating a garden in your backyard. If you want a different result in life, you have to change what you're doing. However, it's important to remember that nothing happens overnight.

Taking action by taking small steps every day will result in massive momentum over time. I've gone through this process many times in my life, and it works. I used to hate running, but I would make myself do it a couple of times a week until I became better at it. I'm not a marathon runner by any stretch, but I know for sure that I can run a 5K at any time and feel great doing it. All it took was me changing my mindset around running and deciding that being a good runner was something I could accomplish. Then, I worked at it little by little until I got there.

The same goes for nutrition. When you first start trying to eat better, it seems impossible to eat only the healthy foods your body needs. But by taking small steps every day, over and over, your body will slowly get used to your new diet and actually start to crave healthy food - plus, you'll feel so much better along the way.

Business and entrepreneurship are the same way. What is the thing that makes you uncomfortable but you know you need to do? For me, it's accounting. I'm a terrible accountant, but I made myself learn. I had to because my business depended on it. Now, my business is thriving, and it's because I made the decision to step out of my comfort zone and take action.

I want you to choose one thing you'll take action on starting this week. Write it down and come up with a game plan of what steps you'll take each day to achieve your goal. Set a timeline and reward yourself when you reach your goal. There's no time better than right now!

CONGRATULATIONS, YOU DID IT!

You learned the importance of launching a personal brand, how to market your brand, become a sales rockstar, build the business and become the best version of yourself so you can live the life you want to live! The most important thing to do now is START! Our team at D2 Branding is here to help you! Go to www.DeedraDeterman.com and click on "Get Started" to get your free consultation on launching your personal brand. I can't wait to ignite your brand to increase your profit so you can live your best life!

Stay in touch with me by watching/listening to the DO IT MY WAY Podcast at www.DoItMyWayPodcast.com or on your favorite podcast app. You can always find us on Facebook, Instagram, LinkedIn and TikTok @D2Branding, @DeedraDeterman and @DOITMYWAY.

My goal with this book was to inspire at least one person to create a personal brand and change their life. If this book has inspired you, I would love to hear your story!

www.ingramcontent.com/pod-product-compliance
Ingram Content Group UK Ltd.
Pitfield, Milton Keynes, MK11 3LW, UK
UKHW021908190726
13853UKWH00002B/575